Outrage!

Man the Myth/Man the Actuality

SPR CHARTER

THE GUILD OF TUTORS PRESS

Also by SPR Charter:

MAN ON EARTH (Grove Press)
'FOR UNTO US A CHILD IS BORN' (Applegate Books)
THE CHOICE AND THE THREAT (Ballantine Books)
THE PLANNING MYTH (Applegate Books)

Other writings and tapes available from:
APPLEGATE BOOKS
Box 22124
San Francisco, CA 94122

First Edition
Copyright © 1978 by SPR Charter
ISBN 0-89615-010-0 — Paper
        0-89615-011-9 — Case
Library of Congress No: 78-059920

Table of Contents

THREE: NEW SCIENTIFIC ETHICS

FOUR: ARE IDEAS IMPRACTICAL?

FIVE: OUR WONDROUS PLANET

SIX: FUTURISTS AND FALLACIES

SEVEN: TECHNOLOGY AND THE WILL OF THE PEOPLE

EIGHT: PLANETARY AND PERSONAL STRESS

TEN: THE LABEL AND THE SUBSTANCE

ELEVEN: ILLUSION AND DELUSION

TWELVE: THOUGHT AND OPINION

THIRTEEN: MAN, THE LIVING END

FOREWORD

At the beginning of our third century we may be thought of as a middle-aged nation beset with many of the fears and self-doubts which fall upon societies and individuals no longer young.

In 1776, at the nation's birth, its founders were informed and sustained by the Age of Reason. Rational men, stimulated by triumphs in mathematics and a materialistic science, had no cause to doubt that Man's control over natural forces could, in time, only lead to the greatest happiness for the greatest number. The troubling paradoxes and complexities of the industrial society still lay far ahead. Even at the end of the first century of the nation's existence (coinciding roughly with the initial hundred years of modern industrial development), although pervasive social and economic inequities had fostered new ideologies (more in Europe, at first, than in the United States), the spirit was still optimistic and faith in rational science as the basis of inevitable progress was largely undiminished.

But now, some two hundred years later, in the United States and throughout the Western world, there is a growing sense of betrayal, a feeling that man, with his technology and his science, has not merely been shaping the environment to his own ends but, all too often misshaping it. As a result those who have concerned themselves at all have largely split into two contending camps — the technophobes and the technophiles — and the discourse between them becomes more contentious and strident with each passing year.

Only rarely do we hear a voice that rises forcefully above the shrillness of technophilia and technophobia to speak to the very core of the issues — back to those first principles which have been silted over by the detritus of the technological centuries. SPR Charter has such a voice and in this book of spare, trenchant essays he continues the lucid soundings that have been the hallmark of his writings for many years.

A decade and a half ago, Aldous Huxley, in his Foreword to Charter's book, MAN ON EARTH, wrote the following:

'"Forgive them, for they know not what they do." But will there be for-
giveness for those who know quite well what they are doing, and how
bad it is, but refuse, nonetheless, to stop? And what about those whose
ignorance is real but voluntary, who don't know and know that they don't
know, but make no serious effort to acquire knowledge and blithely
persist in criminally idiotic courses of action which they can always excuse
after the disastrous event by protesting they really had no idea . . .? . . .

. . . It is the great merit of Charter's book that it compels us to ask such
questions — as members of Earth's dominant species, are we interested
in survival and, hopefully, the improvement of Homo sapiens? Or are we
doing our best to accelerate Man's extinction or, at the least, his deca-
dence and dehumanisation? . . .'

That book was a call to renewal and a rededication to the beginnings of a design theory for Man.

Dr. Charter's faith in Man's potential has never flagged, I believe,
even as he has contemplated with searching clarity the possibility of
human extinction; and now, in *Outrage!* he suggests that we could
be approaching a new Golden Age of Man. This is not at all in the
sense of Utopian abundance (indeed if that were our hope it would
be foredoomed) but rather of an awakening to our unexplored
capacity for ethical evolvement.

What would be needed? For one thing, a recognition that scientific objectivity, as it is practiced today, is a myth; and if scientists
truly wish to make free choices then ethics, morality and aesthetics
must once again become part of their system of thought. For
another, an understanding that Man is a unique species with
special and awesome responsibilities. Unlike the Lorentzes and
the Ardreys, Charter does not confuse analogy with homology.
For yet another, an acceptance that 'human nature' is changeable
— not fixed — and capable of transcendence beyond the moment.
Above all there must be a recognition that this is a planet of 4,000-
million individual human beings — each of whom has an insepara-
ble relationship to eternity, to every other individual, and to the
limited Earth.

This is wisdom redeemed — it is nothing less than a philosophy
for a new age.

RALPH PARKMAN
San Jose State University

AUTHOR'S NOTE

In each of us, as we surely know by now, good cohabits with evil and the noble with the sinister.

Since The Bomb and the ensuing explosion in our technical knowledge and competence, our capabilities have become sinister indeed, even those originally intended for beneficial purposes: genetic 'engineering,' weather modification, electronic surveillance, to name a few, have quickly developed into actualities full of foreboding.

The individual human being has always expressed his or her 'noble' side through creative ability to pursue an idea in all its complex evolvement. Each of us has a personal viewing plateau constantly changing from which we can try to see ourselves and gain a perspective on our place in the Universe. For each of us this plateau exists only in the ongoing present.

Within this present — perhaps as a withdrawal from the edge of the precipice of our own making — an awakening unique in history seems to be taking place all over the world: an awakening to the value of life and of this planet; to the irretrievability of certain aspects of life; to a sense of responsibility to the future as well as to the now. It is as yet a small awakening as of the opening of only one eye; but the stirrings are there. Perhaps it has come about through the information-explosion.

But facts and data-collections, of themselves, are no longer sufficient to give meaning to our increasing knowledge. Mere knowledge without a deepening awareness of uncovered interrelationships is dangerous, even as awareness without knowledge is sterile.

Though the good, the noble, the truly creative within all of us cohabits with the evil and the sinister, and the latter now often appears to be dominant, no individual person considers himself or herself to be irretrievable. That we shall not become so is the reason for this book.

I believe in the invincibility of the human spirit and in its ability to rectify mistakes. Aware of the peril of our position, many older people are devoting themselves to this now. Many of the young are searching.

These short essays do not pretend to say all that should be said on their various subjects; their intent is to wake the reader to open both his eyes to his or her own thoughts and visions regarding Man-the-Myth and Man-the-Actuality.

SPR CHARTER

OUTRAGE

Man the Myth/Man the Acutality

A COMMENT ON CYNICISM
. . . it is difficult to be 'realistic' . . .

At one time, when life was relatively secure and the future not so much in doubt, when the world had a larger absorptive capacity for all sorts of things than it does now, cynicism was considered an eccentric view containing satirical humour which could be readily and engagingly absorbed. It expressed trenchant wit, irony or sarcasm for the purpose of exposing and discrediting human vice or folly. It was often an *active* reflection of a pessimism quite different from the deadening passivity of depression. Today cynicism is used in a cruel contemptuous manner to describe the human descent; and public cynicism in the name of 'realism' is increasingly being accepted by people who have become disenchanted and distrustful toward their world and themselves.

Of course it is difficult to be 'realistic' in our perpetually perishing world without becoming cynical to self, whether harshly or genteelly, in nearly all areas of our response. Yet all bitter beliefs, even in sum, are only part of 'realism'; they are not the whole of realism because the human capability for realism itself covers a vast spectrum, and not only a narrow band. To limit this spectrum to only one segment in the name of 'realism' is, quite realistically, a self-mutilation and equivalent to self-limiting our grand and subtle visible spectrum to only various shades of blue.

At one time the ancient philosophical school of Cynics taught that virtue is the only good, and that the essence of the good lies in self-control and independence. But words — especially those relating to thought — often have their meanings changed in time, even as the human condition changes. Actually, the change in the meanings of historic words is a potent indicator of our own changed thoughts and responses. Not at all parenthetically: While language is one of our living attributes, it does not always evolve with time; it may, and often does, devolve. This too is a potent indicator of where we are which we disregard at our own peril.

Today we feel that our world has become humourless and so saturated with the bad that cynicism is no longer satirical but an expression of a debilitating frame-of-mind. It is now self-devouring, toxic, virulent, poisonous and vituperative; and the public cynic now panders to people's fears, bitter depressions, and to their lowest levels of response. When cynicism becomes prevalent in so many people it becomes a pestilence. When we retain and extoll cynicism we may never emerge from those causes which brought us to the bitterness of cynicism, and to deadening depression.

And yet, to be cynical in certain ways is now virtually unavoidable. Indeed, a few cynics expressing satiricalness are very much needed in our world. We need cynics with trenchant wit, irony and sarcasm to expose to us and to discredit many of the follies and even vices of, for instance, those commercial gurus of the good who, for proper entrance fees, offer packaged instant insight or primal raucousness or incense-filled costly quietude to troubled minds and spirits of those of diluted dependence upon their inner selves. And there are so many such people in the world. For myself, I am quite cynical of such cult-peddlers, but I am far more compassionate than cynical toward their followers of troubled minds and spirits however gulled they may be.

━━━━━━━━━━━━

FAITH AS A HUMAN CONSTANT
. . . this ancient organic need . . .

The loss of faith is very costly to the individual who is left anchorless, especially now, when so many of us feel a sense of frustration and impotence in our confrontation with so many man-made factors which lead to personal uncertainties, even despairs.

Each of us needs a belief in something larger than self in order to lend substance to our lives and to our sense of purpose and future. This need is a human constant so long as people retain humaneness and individuality. It is through this ancient organic need that, in my view, the human concept of Deity emerged as one of mankind's greatest innovations.

From earliest times this concept of Deity was taken over and administered by priestly classes which subjected the populace, through fear and promise, to different rituals for the 'correct' service of their beliefs. While great organised religions flourished for many centuries, in our present world the religions are fading — yet the need for belief in something larger than self remains.

One of the many reasons why the established religions are failing is, in my view, the fact that religion itself has become displaced as a fountainhead of faith; a displacement which organised religion has been bringing upon itself for many decades and for many reasons — basically because religion itself has proven to be without much guidance and hope for both Man and Earth. Organised religion has become so externalised, and people in increasing numbers reject both its promises and its threats.

Man's faith is now more in his devices than in his belief in organised religion, or in a God. But our devices are also proving to be quite insufficient for our faith because so many of them fail, so many are replaceable, so many seem to be quite pointless.

Yet to be without faith is to be adrift within self, much less within the world and the Cosmos, with no references through which to know our own selves, and through which to learn something of our own perspectives and our own largenesses. After all, life cannot live in any sort of vacuum.

Today, precisely because of the vacuum of faith, a plethora of cultist groups — each maintaining that it is the truer container of faith than any other — seeks adherents to various beliefs and rituals. Their people speak rather mechanically of 'the spirituality of all things,' and to me they seem to be not pantheistic so much as what religious people used to term, pejoratively, paganistic and heathenish — people without faith but with much ritual. And these groups are very much like our devices: many of them fail, many are replaceable, many seem to be quite pointless, and some quite obviously are harmful through their destructive consumption of individuality and humaneness of those they entice to become followers.

And yet this concern with 'spirituality,' 'awareness,' 'consciousness' could be such a very good thing if only the people within these groups were not so regimented, so rigid in their beliefs, so pious in their religiosities. Nevertheless, the fact itself that there is a concern with spirituality is an indication of some sort of awakening.

It is indeed true that Man needs a different idea of himself, a different faith, not in *confrontation* with the immensity within him, and also external to him, but in interrelationship with this immensity. Confrontation is often an antagonism; interrelationship is often a cohesion. We need faith, individual faith, that we are still capable of grasping the actuality of human largeness within self which extends beyond self, beyond the now, in our often stumbling attempts to ascend from the caves of our own making, guided by our own clarities of what we are and by our own visions of what we may yet become.

A HUMAN ASSUMPTION
. . . *we need to make basic qualitative changes* . . .

For a long time my work has been based upon the assumption that life will continue on Earth into the long foreseeable future. This is a human assumption for which there can be no demonstrable proof in the present.

An opposite assumption torsions our sanity and amputates our hope. It also denies to us the basic biological fact which has been a reality since the earliest beginnings of life: that life seeks to live, not to die. However, because of our technological interferences, even for the good, in many biological processes involving life and death, being and existence, this reality is no longer any assurance of our continuation. Whatever assurances we seek now need to emerge from our human capabilities.

Nevertheless, despite lack of proof and assurance, let us accept for now the unprovable assumption, and also our need to strengthen and act upon it.

Given the basic assumption that human life will indeed continue on this planet, we can project from where we now stand at least one of the essential conditions without which this assumption becomes totally invalid:

If human life is to continue we need to make basic qualitative changes in our selves—not in one dramatic sweep, which would be impossible, but in a series of incremental changes some of which are already taking place.

A qualitative change is that which modifies at least one of our own basic frames-of-reference and, thereby, our way-of-life. A quantitative change is one which reinforces or weakens our frames-of-reference but does not alter our way-of-life. For instance: When we see our *selves* in the hungry war-torn child, our way of viewing our selves and the child is altered qualitatively. When we see the child as only one of many, our compassion may be increased quantitatively in terms of our assistance, or even be decreased quantitatively to impotence because we see that there are so many such children. Another example of the difference between quantitative and qualitative change can be drawn from the elementary chemical distinction between a mixture and a compound. In a chemical mixture the ingredients can readily be separated into its unchanged component parts. In a compound the ingredients are so joined as to form a substance of quite a different quality from its original components.

If we are concerned over the human continuation we simply must become more qualitative in evaluating our thoughts and subsequent actions. This simple statement obtains from whatever perspective we approach the hope for our continuation. However, from this statement many complexities emerge, as expected. One of them is indeed the question *What is Man for?* for which no answer can even be attempted without wondering whether there is an 'ingredient' present and available within our own evolvement which moves 'human nature' upward, so to speak, so that it is 'human' indeed to give substance to the expectation that life will continue on our planet.

POIGNANT CONTRADICTIONS
. . . to be human is to be many things . . .

We are in a world of unbelievable beauty, of breath-holding moments; and a world of unbelievable ugliness. A world of unbelievable riches and unbelievable poverty; of unbelievable life-givingness and death-dealingness. And we are the only organisms — we as individuals are the only organisms — capable of wending our way through these poignant contradictions and of trying to make sense of our selves within this growing maze of contradictions.

Imagine if you will the grandeur within such a capability! and the abiding strength within it for each of us. This capability offers hope that we are not condemned by the contradictions. Our individual spirit can be nourished by this capability; our sense of potency can be stimulated by it; our intimate sense of our own life and the lives of others close to us can be enriched by it. But we need to recognise and embrace the existence within us of this capability, and cherish it as a precious human gift which we dare not allow to recede from us or to be encrusted by us. And it does fade from us when we do not nourish it as a reality within our own lives.

Surely each of us prefers beauty to ugliness, riches to poverty in all their aspects; and life to death. Yet too often we function as though the opposites were our preferences.

To be human is to be many things, one of which is to be capable of response, of the deepest response possible to us, to that which is all about us within our own 'reality.' How we interpret this reality to our selves, how we see our selves within what we consider to be reality to us, is so very much to the point here.

Consider the flight of a bird and the smile of a child; the birth of yet another day for us and the reality of its irretrievability . . . part of the poetry of life. But in order to 'read' it we must be literate, so to speak — not in words alone but especially in insight and interpretation. We need to know the many languages of life, both spoken and unspoken.

Gods are simple to understand; they are always 'good.' Devils are simple to understand; they are always 'evil.' They contain neither contradictions nor a capability for selectivity. Gods and devils have no choices to be anything but what they are. Their attributes are fixed for all time—and by us because we have set them.

We, however, do contain both contradictions *and* selectivity. Each of us is a selective being in that we are capable of exercising personal choices in many areas of our intimate response to the reality all about us; we still retain this capability in quite some measure. We, and only we as individuals, can bless the birth of yet another of our days on Earth and cherish its irretrievable pre-ciousness.

While each of us sees reality in a way different from another, only we to our selves are capable of seeing our own reality to our selves and of interpreting it for our selves, positively or negatively, hopefully or despairingly, within our increasing contradictions.

THE NOBLE AND THE SINISTER
. . . an awakening unique in all our history . . .

We are not born with wisdom but only with the capability to seek it in the lifelong processes of our own evolvement. We can be the noblest of creatures on Earth, yet we have always had our sinister side cohabiting with our noble side.

Since The Bomb and the ensuing explosion in our technical knowledge and competence our capabilities have become very sinister indeed. Even those capabilities originally conceived for beneficial purposes—genetic 'engineering,' weather modification, electronic surveillance, and so many others—have quite quickly become capabilities and actualities full of foreboding for both us and our Earth.

However, we also always have had our noble side expressed through our creativity and our capability to pursue the Ideal; a capability expressible by the individual through his or her pursuit of idea and its complex evolvement.

We each have our own viewing plateau which is constantly changing as *we* rise and fall, and from which we try to perceive our selves and to grasp some perspective of our own place within immensity, within the vastness of our own personal universe. This changing plateau — without which we cannot locate our own bearings — this platform exists for each of us only within our ongoing present.

Within this present, and perhaps as a drawing back from the brink of the precipices of our own making, an awakening unique in all our history seems to be taking place over the land and indeed within peoples throughout the world — perhaps it is a small awakening akin to the opening of only one eye at first. Yet it is a stirring of awakening to the preciousness and uniqueness of life and of this our only Earth, and to the irretrievability of many aspects of life; an awakening to a sense of responsibility to the future as well as to the now; an awakening to a self-consciousness of responsibility never before experienced on such a broad scale in all our history.

These stirrings may well be a partial result of the ongoing explosion of information.

But data, facts, are of themselves no longer sufficient to lend meaning to our increasing knowledge. Indeed, knowledge without ongoing deepening awareness of uncovered and uncoverable inter-relationships is dangerous, even as awareness without knowledge is sterile. And indeed too, both knowledge and awareness are incremental to each of us. When we reject the incremental as an essential and unavoidable ingredient in our own processes of gaining knowledge and awareness, and want to accept only that which is instantly and easily available to us full blown, the first pebble we confront becomes to us a boulder, and the boulder a mountain and we've nightmares of our effectiveness.

We need to awaken *our selves*, to open both our eyes, to our own visions and our own thoughts of the ongoing actuality that while the sinister within us cohabits with our creative capability to seek the Ideal, so long as we possess and nurture this capability and continue seeking both knowledge and awareness we do not become irretrievable to ourselves.

CREATIVITY AND SEMINAL IDEA
. . . *the artesian wellspring* . . .

A seminal idea is that which Man creates—which Man-the-Individual creates—and which both leads us to, and exposes us as individuals to, the multiple Universes within us, within which we discover and re-discover for ourselves the multiple meanings to us of existence. Seminal idea, throughout all of Man's history, has been and remains the artesian wellspring of his emergence and ascent. Each generation must discover for itself both the need for seminal idea and the need for its seeking; when it does not, the wellspring becomes silted and the generation falters.

Creativity is not, in itself, a seminal idea because, in actuality, creativity exists within each of us in varying degrees; we do not 'create' creativity, so to speak, although we become aware of it in many ways both gross and subtle in our attempts to function within it as individuals. It is out of creativity that seminal ideas may emerge.

Creativity, in its most simple expression, is the biological necessity for the continuum of life because life seeks life, not death. This applies to all living matter, both plants and animals. Plants are the most instinctive here; and animals are far more instinctive here than the human organism which has modified, manipulated, glorified, degraded and enhanced this primitive creative expression which exists within all living things and beings.

As Man evolved within the evolutionary entwinings of his growing mind/body/spiritual/emotional complexity, his necessity for creativity also evolved with increasing complexity. Possessing a growing capability for expressing himself—a capability without which he would not have been able to survive in his world which was not at all amenable to him *unless* he evolved—in his evolvement Man's need became urgent to express his astonishment and his fear, his admiration and his amazement, of his world. (Are we losing this urgency?)

In his evolvement Man became capable of deliberate projectability beyond the moment; and his roots of creativity became ever stronger and more nourishing to him in his need to place his world in order, so to speak. In all of Nature chaos is discomfitting—and

Man is always and forever part of Nature and never apart from it. Within chaos the human essentiality for projectability becomes disrupted and the human evolvement founders. And within chaos the human need for creativity may become a virtual inner agony in his inner search for a sense of order and meaning in his universe.

Creativity generates within us that sense of roots and belonging without which we would indeed be the Children of Chaos, the lost in the night. And it is out of the deepest implications of creativity that seminal ideas may indeed emerge. And it is through seminal idea that the tangible and the intangible merge in that union so essential for our further evolvement.

THE DOOMSDAY ATLAS
. . . it is our necessity to climb the mountain . . .

The Pentagon has a revised Doomsday Atlas that shows Americans where not to be in the event of a nuclear war; it shows, in effect, that Americans, in that eventuality, should not be in America.

Each of us functions in many ways through our own frames-of-reference — as do our institutions and their controllers. The Pentagon's frame-of-reference is planning of deliberate massive death of millions — and its mirror-image, which is the attempted avoidance of massive death through massive retaliative power. Death and anti-death through retaliative power is its frame-of-reference. The Soviet equivalent to the Pentagon surely has an equivalent frame-of-reference.

That the two most massive Powers on our planet are so deeply immersed in planning of death — and anti-death through more death — as a matter of policy is more than only tragic; it is violently insane, especially in the face of growing awareness by individuals throughout the world of the finiteness of our planet, and of its commonality, so to speak, for all life.

The Doomsday Atlas, in whatever language it is presented, is yet another tangible manifestation of the incremental bad enveloping our world since The Bomb. Is it too late for us all? Must we accept such atlases as the maps of our lives? Must absurdity, and surreal horror too, now become *our* frame-of-reference? And, so much to the point, are such questions now pointless?

NO! They are now so very much to the point that one of the ultimate tragedies we confront (and we are now in a world of many ultimate tragedies) is for us to accept as the 'reality' of our lives that we can now no longer ask these questions as our human and humane right because it is too late for us or because we are now powerless when in confrontation with these questions, and with the power-policies which give rise, full-blown, to such questions.

Many things in our world have changed in the recent past, things both good and bad. There is surely a broader awakening among people to the reality that our institutions are not worthy of our blind trust; that our elected and appointed officials function from frames-of-reference too far distant and hazy from our own to lend substantive meaning to our individual lives. These questions — unasked a decade or so ago except by the very few — are part of the awakening processes. To expect an instant change for the good, and to despair when it does not happen in the instant, is indeed to relinquish the map of our own lives to Pentagonorrheaic Doomsday Atlases presented in the many languages of power to a populace being bent into acceptance and even submission.

While this is a brooding gloomy thought, my point here is not to dig a deeper hole at the foot of Mt. Everest in order to make the climb to sanity higher and, thereby, more rewarding. I have thought again and again: Why present unpalatabilities? Why not present only those things which will lower the mountain — not raise it. But the mountain remains, and we neither lower it nor raise it. We raise or lower our selves. It is our necessity to climb the mountain — in this analogy — which is the vital factor; not because it is *there*, but because we are *here*. And for this ascent we need to prepare ourselves, and to remain steadfastly prepared in many ways — especially internally within our selves — both to realise the difficulty of the climb and, even more, to be able to recognise the ledges available to us in our attempted ascent to sanity. And even more yet, to know with a reality surpassing despair that we are to ourselves an organic unity seeking life and not rubble-strewn falls into the void. *This* surpassing reality is indeed now one of the basic challenges—and abiding strengths too—of our individual selves.

And whether or not those in present attempts do achieve sanity, we can as we must transmit to other and later climbers the knowledge, difficulties and, yes, occasional exhuberances encountered, and to do so with hope and expectation that others, standing as we all do upon the shoulders of all the past, will continue as a necessity of *their* lives the everlasting *attempted* ascents toward sanity.

ON THE CONSUMPTION OF THE SEED
. . . *what kind of harvest will we reap for our wintering . . .?*

Try to imagine the fortitude, the dilemma, of a tribal people with their winter larder totally bare except for a cache of seeds. Try to imagine starving parents watching their starving children, then looking again and again at the seeds they know will soon be needed for springtime planting.

What would *you* do? What alternatives do you have? If you do not eat the seeds you have saved for planting you will die soon. If you eat them you will die later because you will have nothing to plant and harvest for next year's wintering.

What, indeed, would you do?

One of the truly tragic calamities which can confront a people, a tribe, is when winter starvation forces them to consume the seeds they have preserved for next year's crop—and, with the coming of planting time, finding themselves with no seeds, no summer growing crop, no autumn food to harvest.

With the coming of spring and summer such a tribe might sustain itself for a while on wild fruits and edible roots and barks and grasses — and even edible animals assuming they could catch them. In their weakened condition the search for food would consume their waking hours. They might try to borrow seeds from a related tribe — and fail. And then the winter cold descends upon them and the land, and starvation, literal starvation, destroys them.

While this is difficult for us to conceive of happening in our world, it has happened often in the past and is happening today. Many have died, and are dying, of starvation because they consumed the seeds they needed for tomorrow.

Faced by starvation, who amongst us has the fortitude and foresight to preserve seeds for tomorrow?

I do not mean only those seeds we put into the ground to grow but those seeds within us from which we reap our later harvests and re-seedings — especially those good seeds planted in us long ago by our human tribe: those seeds of honour, justice, dignity, integrity, love, compassion, hope — you know the words, the names of the seeds. They have not been forgotten. Not yet.

How many of these seeds have we already consumed so there can be no re-planting, no harvesting, no winter sustenance, no possible re-seeding? How many are we now in process of consuming? How many, without foresight, are we preparing to consume now? All of them?

Land, air, water — our life-sustaining and life-generating resources — we are consuming them too. What will replace them? When we have consumed the living seeds and their sustaining resources, what kind of harvest will we reap for our wintering? And what of the intangible seeds so hugely vital to life?

ON 'SPIRIT' AND 'SPIRITUALITY'
. . . the organic and the synthetic . . .

When all about us we see life duplicating itself so endlessly—in humans and flowers, trees and birds—fully to grasp and comprehend, and appreciate, the nature and significance of our own finite individual existences is very difficult indeed.

I believe there is a growing hunger of the spirit in people which the many current facades of 'spirituality' cannot assuage.

Even in our contemporary technological world with its huge data-piles and mountains of retrievable answers in need of basic questions, someone may speak of the 'spirit of the tree' and not be dismissed as an out-of-date romantic. All living things do contain a 'spirit' to the individual to whom the *ingredient* of spirit is essential.

Spirit to me is both an adjective and a verb, as well as a noun. It is the will to live, and the majestic personification of that will to live. In gravely sick patients this will to live, this spirit, is accepted by attending physicians as a valuable medical reality; each of us has surely noted more than one blade of grass emerging from the concrete in which its seed was imbedded; even acorns planted in pots placed in dark corners will upon occasion attempt to sprout, however gnarled the emerging seedling may be. There is a reality for all to see as 'spirit' in this majestic personification of the will to live. One does not need to be 'highly educated' to be able to see and experience the 'spirit' of Earth and all its offspring. Children, for instance, are far more intuitive here. Indeed, the education to which we are now subjected is more often a deterrent than an asset to such understanding.

Despite the disturbing discordancy we can see all about us there is the inescapable realisation of the preciousness and uniqueness of all things possessing life—of their chance *only once* to have *their* life (whether bird or child or weed or tree) no matter how short or tenuous or difficult. The indomitable spirit of all living things to grasp their once-ness at life is gallant and poignant to an observer in the same predicament, as all of us are in one way or another.

'Spirituality,' however, is something else again. There are so many false facades of what is called 'spirituality' now abounding in packaged forms, and cleverly merchandised to those in want of ease and comfort when they confront the puzzle of their lives. As now used, the word 'spirituality' has become exploitive.

The difference between spirit and spirituality is, in many ways, the difference between the organic and the synthetic. Spirit is individually organic to all life; 'spirituality,' as the word is now used, is an increasingly synthetic mass-product for the marketplace.

In its basic meaning spirituality does indeed exist — but only, it seems to me, in the beholder and perhaps only in retrospective awareness. When a person is deliberately aware of his 'spirituality,' the probabilities are that it is not only self-congratulatory and much too self-conscious but also quite diluted and faded. For instance, people who say that they are 'into spirituality' (such a curious expression) may quite easily the next day be 'into' macramé.

To me spirituality is transient within the moment or many moments, and it cannot ever be a static state within one's existence. Spirituality is incremental after years of observation, contemplation, acceptance and understanding of multiplicities of *spirit*; it is a flash of awareness within an individual, followed by another flash, and another and another — all of which gradually create the recognition, in conscious awareness, of the union of all the multiple aspects of life.

<hr>

THE 'ECOLOGICAL IMPERATIVE'
. . . we all share the same destiny . . .

Has an 'ecological imperative' always existed on our Earth — imperative in the sense of action or responsibility not to be avoided or evaded? I rather doubt that.

With the beginnings of life certain conditions came into being, certain inter-twinings developed, and a web of life formed within which cause-and-effect relationships obtained. And the planet at that time contained a huge absorptive capability. As the web became more complex, species indeed became extinct and for many reasons, but Earth's absorptive capacity absorbed the extinctions and the web of life continued.

Man's emergence and manipulations of the planet gradually rent this web of life. Simultaneously, Earth's absorbability gradually lessened. It is only in comparatively recent times—when Man thought he could remove himself from all of Nature and all of the web of life—that Man's manipulations began to reach the critical mass, so to speak, and that Earth's absorbability began to reach the saturation-point. It is then that an ecological imperative of our own making came into inevitable existence, precisely in the sense of action and responsibility not to be avoided or evaded.

Yet this imperative is not some idol to be worshipped or some 'ism' which will solve all our problems. It is not even a point-of-view because points-of-view cause separations into pigeonholes of varying size and reach; and whatever our point-of-view may be, we are beginning dimly to perceive that we—Man and all living things —all share the same destiny in this interrelated world which we are making increasingly interrelated. And the ecological imperative, precisely because we all do share the same destiny, the same web-of-life, is indeed to us, as manipulators, an imperative. This imperative, which we have brought about, is equivalent to our having added another letter to our alphabet, thereby expanding and surely modifying our meanings, capabilities, and responsibilities for as long as 'forever' is to us.

Consider the reality that one of our human gifts is our capability for non-linear non-sequential thinking, which we all do. I believe that we are quite actually incapable of possessing within our minds only one solitary thought at any given time; even the simplest of our minds is much too complex for that. Nevertheless, in our actions, and our plans for actions, we are indeed linear and sequential. Our actions and our minds seem to be not at all in harmony. In our actions we constantly look for orders-of-priority as guides to our capabilities. The belief in 'first things first' has dominated our capabilities for centuries, and especially so since the beginnings of industrialisation, of mechanisation; and even more so within our present computerised age.

If first things indeed come first, and second things second, then last things come last — if there is time and energy for them. Nevertheless, in terms of interweavings, of interrelationships, there can be no such gradations or orders-of-priority. One cannot weave anything, anything at all, gown or shroud, with only one thread; and much less the tapestry of life.

The ecological imperative — indeed of our own making and which we ignore at our own peril — demands of us our increasing recognition and willing acceptance of our need to *do* not only this but also that; to *think* of not only this but also that — simultaneously, if ever our capabilities and our minds are to exist harmoniously within us as individuals; and if ever we and our progeny are to continue to exist, much less to evolve upon this planet. And we cannot live if other life does not also live with us — simultaneously.

The ecological imperative is in life seeking to live, not to die; in life's imperative to establish harmony within existence. Our capability deliberately to generate ecological discord, and to rationalise the discord, is a stupid rejection of this imperative. And in such rejection we become dinosauric — that is, extinctive — in both our actions and our thoughts — also simultaneously.

IS DELIBERATE VIOLENCE ORGANIC TO US?
. . . with our unique capacity for reason . . .

There are many aspects of violence: national, international, revolutionary, group, institutional, and personal violence. And also what we call 'natural violence,' the violence of Nature: storms, lightning-caused forest fires, earthquakes, and so on — phenomena we consider in our human interpretation of such events to be Nature's 'violence.'

Within the context of this brief comment, violence refers to that which is man-made, and to that which is an overt deliberate malevolent againstism, so to speak; it is deliberate human action against self, other people, institutions. The opposite of violence, within this context, is not non-violence but reason.

Is deliberate malevolent violence organic to us, genetically? If it is, increasing violence in all its manifestations is then inevitable for mankind: violence in the streets, violence as a basic tool of power, a weapons-ridden world, are then our actualities as well as our expectations. And the devices for malevolent violence, on all levels, are today literally horrendous and becoming more so. Our acceptance of violence as being inherent to us conditions us into accepting ever greater expenditures of self, nations, Earth-resources for ever greater capabilities for violence. Those who believe that violence is organic to us also believe that as our capabilities increase so does our violence, inevitably. Increasing violence — and preparations for violence — then have a genetic justification, so to speak, which we cannot overcome readily, however good our intentions to do so may be.

Reason itself is then not only weakened as a positive uniquely human attribute but it can function for the good only as a constraint to our organic violence.

However, it may very well be that violence is an acquired, not a genetic characteristic built upon incrementally until it has become part of the acculturation processes of mankind. If so, we are surely not doomed to increasing violence as the way of our lives.

Consider the reality that Man is a biological organism, and that biological organisms are not deliberately violent, as Nature is not deliberately violent — or non-violent. We are part of Nature, always, with a unique capacity for reason. Our deliberate malevolent violence is basically anti-Nature and, thereby, imposed upon us by our selves incrementally through the reduction of reason to the degree where it is very nearly impossible for us to imagine a world without human violence.

From its earliest beginnings religion, for instance, with its promises and its good-and-evil polarised foundations has much to account for in violence. Contemporary technology with *its* promises also has much to account for within the context of learned incremental violence. We do violence to Earth — and in the name of the goodlife — through our technological excesses and pollutions and, thereby, do violence to our selves and future generations. How can such violence even be thought of as being organic to us?

The promises of technology were themselves misdirections from the very beginning, and we are now paying the costs of these misdirections of reason. Incremental violence is one of the costs — of the increasing costs — of these misdirections, as the cornucopia becomes emptied of promised abundance. The technological promises of a material goodlife may well be unfulfillable — a possibility so very difficult for us to grasp, yet one from which we need to begin to learn something of the realities of the Man/Earth interrelationship upon which all human life is founded.

If we could recognise the constraints and the grandeurs — and the human responsibilities — of the Man/Earth interrelationship, and absorb them in our bones from infancy, we would know that violence is an incremental conditioning against which we can, as we must, de-condition ourselves; and that the opposite of violence is indeed reason. Once again, this long everlasting process of Education should have begun so much earlier in the human ascent. And if it does not begin today, another day is lost to us — and then another year, and then another generation.

To rationalise violence as being inevitably organic to us is to reject the human *capability* for evolvement. Who amongst us can accept, with submission, this belief and retain sanity?

WHALES AND CATTLE
. . . we need to find emotional excuses . . .

'If the killing of whales is pitiful, why is the killing of cattle not also considered pitiful?' This question was offered as a debatable argument by the president of the Japan Whaling Association; and it is a question asked by other people not economically associated with the killing of whales. It is a question more in need of evaluation than of rebuttal, which describes an attempt at repulsing an opponent's evidence and argument.

First off: Whales are wild creatures of Nature; cattle are tamed domesticated creatures bred by us for food. But there is far more to it than that. We *hunt* wild creatures, we do not hunt the tamed. We slaughter them. (Parenthetically, the more 'tamed' Man becomes, the more we slaughter our own kind.)

Hunting was once a matter of survival-necessity for nearly all people, as it remains today for some, and it may become so again for many people, unfortunately. But hunting for profit is equivalent to the bounty-hunters of the recent past when, even then, they were not held in high repute by their contemporaries. And why not? I believe that the pitting of human skills against creatures incapable of self-protection against us is something we feel, even inarticulately, to be somewhat demeaning *of us*.

By the use of currently sophisticated devices: remote sensing units, helicopters, high-speed chase-boats, automated rendering of carcasses, and so on . . . whales are no longer hunted, but slaughtered. Even those who may hold some regard for the hunter hold little for the slaughterer. The recognition of challenge is a uniquely human attribute, and virtually meaningless to the slaughterer. And the elimination of one uniquely human attribute adversely affects other such attributes.

The whale has become endangered through overkill; and we have all over the world stockpiles of *over*-overkill. Do we not yet realise that overkill has become a matter of national policy for many countries? There is more than one interrelationship between endangered species and endangered Man.

An American Congressman was quoted as saying that '. . . The Soviets even use sperm-whale-oil to lubricate their deadly intercontinental missiles. It is the ultimate irony (he said) that this great animal, second only to Man in intelligence, is dying to serve the nuclear arms race.'

Yes, it is ironic indeed, but not the ultimate irony which, to me, is in the fact that we need to find emotional excuses, so to speak, for saving the whale. The USA may not be using whale-oil for its missiles, and the Soviets may find a better replacement at some point; yet the irony continues. And whether or not the whale is 'second only to Man in intelligence' is not the basic issue. If intelligence is to be the determiner of preservation, we are in more difficulties than we believe we are now. *People* are 'dying to serve the nuclear arms race'; vision is being clouded because of this 'race'; future itself is being foreshortened.

Once again, as seems to be happening with greater frequency in people of the good, as with this Congressman in this instance, the basic issue is missed by the persuaders of the good.

A QUESTION OF HUMAN EXTINCTION
. . . *whether or not Man will endure* . . .

Will Man as a species become extinct on Earth and if so why? and if not, why not?

This is a question that rises off people's consciousness from time to time, and in many of us is always subconsciously present as we try to find meaning in our lives. While the question, when it rises, may seem simple it affects all our thoughts and hopes and actions, and our individual sense of present relationship with Earth and with our attitudes toward the Man/Earth interrelationship which are transmissible only through us.

Time, in a cosmic sense, is virtually beyond human grasp. Therefore, the question of whether or not Man as a species will become extinct on Earth in the graspable future can be asked only in human terms if it is to have an understandable meaning needed for our evolving capabilities. Because answers in our technological world are so abundant we seem to believe that we no longer need to identify basic questions. It is as though we are euphorically adrift on a sea of computerised readouts, uncaring that questions of our existence are beacons without which we continue to remain without guidance for our various voyages.

One of these beacons is: Are we, as individuals, and are those who govern us through controlled governmental and corporate institutions, presently hastening our extinction, or are we and they devoting our enormous capabilities to the extension of our species-life and its further evolvement? In this sense the question of whether or not Man as a species will endure becomes intimate and agonising. And yet, to our detriment, it is a question most of us (especially world leaders and those considered to be the knowledge-able and the wise) do not bother to explore except in passing, while taking expedient measures to stay alive today. Yet even the asking of this question can lead us toward the greatest enhance-ment of life of which we are capable — in fact, toward sanity.

This question is quite different in quality and degree from the basic one which motivated the Committee of Rome studies of the 'limits of growth.' To this Committee and its studies the question was, and remains, essentially a technological one based on the limitations and eventual exhaustion of tangible resources of our limited planet. But for this question to have meaning a philosoph-ical 'input,' so to speak, is also required. Each of us, from the most primitive tribesman to the most advanced theoretical physicist, is a philosophical being in some degree — each of us incapable of erasing, totally and permanently, from our minds those questions of 'Why?'

And yet our present actions on a global scale, affecting each of us *now*, indicate that we are without doubt hastening our own extinction. Already, at this moment, we are well within such man-made processes.

I am not referring to the literal starvation of millions of indi-viduals which is now a growing fact of our lives, or to the ever-widening recognition that our Earth's present and foreseeable food-production simply cannot feed the world's growing popula-tion if present power-policies are continued. Although our accep-tance of them does extinguish something that is humane within us, I am referring to those man-made horrors which can and will make us extinct as a species.

In the USA, the USSR, in China, and now in India too, thou-sands of acres of Earth are already poisoned for human use for many centuries, and the poisoning continues to spread through the use of burial places for nuclear waste which remains poisonous for hundreds, thousands, and hundreds of thousands of years.

The ozone layer of our atmosphere, which protects us and our necessary vegetation against the toxic ultraviolet segment of our sunlight, is pierced again and again, increasingly, by supersonic military and civilian aircraft, and by fluorine-based aerosols. The oceans are in process of dying *now*. And all this in the name of man-made 'progress.'

Again and again the reader has heard of these endangerments — why mention them still again? Because, in my view, these endangerments are increasingly undergoing qualitative changes.

Why are we hastening toward the extinction of our own species?

There is no simple answer to this haunting question. But there is an ingredient which all attempted answers must contain in common, yet which all continue to omit in common. This ingredient continues to be absent from the simplest attempt to the most complex computerised attempt even to begin to answer this question of *Why?*

The essential ingredient to every attempted answer, a beacon to all our searches, is the actual and philosophical question: *What is Man for?* Both in terms of our tangibilities and intangibilities, this is the basic inerasable core of all other questions of human existence and potentiality.

What is human life and all life *for?*

INTELLIGENCE AND DESTRUCTIVENESS
. . . *the imprecision of wisdom* . . .

Man's intelligence, in its evolvement, leads him ever-closer to terminal destruction, to his own termination. The Bomb is one example here; another is the rising manipulative genetic threat now present within microbiology, even though many consider such manipulation to be a promise. While the counting of blessings is indeed a pleasant pursuit, today one threat, if effective, can be terminal; and from the execution of that threat there is no return.

Man leads himself to terminal destruction not because of a built-in genetic 'lemming factor'; it is not because he seeks death as a release. It is because he does not seek life as the precious unique gift it is. It is a 'lemming factor' by default.

And why is this so? And need it be so?

So long as Man's intelligence rejects the essentiality to him of a philosophical basis *for* his intelligence, his intelligence will inevitably lead to his terminal destruction. This was always so in the long ascent of Man. But not until three decades ago — not until The Bomb which added another letter to our alphabet thereby modifying all of the human future — was his destructive capability actually, literally, terminal toward himself and all life. And it is precisely during this period that philosophy has fallen into greater disrepute than ever before; that philosophy has been so electronically, so technologically, manipulated by those who turned it into private gain in terms of structures of sectisms.

The reality confronts us with haunting unavoidability that Man's intelligence — when not based upon and stemming from his philosophical essentialities in terms of ethics, morality, aesthetics, when not based upon his recognised need for wisdom, inevitably leads him to terminal destruction.

Are we then prisoners of our own intelligence? of our own raceways? Have we neither free will nor choice here?

To choose to live or to die is a choice of personal paucity.

At one time 'scientific objectivity' was part of the best processes of scientific inquiry. Today the term 'scientific objectivity' has become a shelter for escaping from the ethical, moral, aesthetic implications and responsibilities of the technological applications proliferating from scientific inquiry. And this has become basically dangerous to us all and to Science itself. How can the most skillful laboratory devotions to potential massive death ever be called Science or be labelled 'scientific objectivity'?

We have choice and free will only in areas of our own creations. For instance: In Science the practitioners can indeed choose to devote themselves to areas which contribute to the good; and, for choice here to be valid, they need to concern themselves with what *is* the good within the context of life and to recognise this context as being unavoidably philosophical and indivisible from Science.

If a 'scientist' (a word now so diluted and misused) is unconcerned with ethics, morality, aesthetics, because he seeks what he calls 'objectivity' divorced from such aspects, he then relinquishes his choice and free will to the myth of 'scientific objectivity,' which is not an actuality. He thereby relinquishes his human responsibility to this myth which governs his efforts and *controls* his choice, and dominates his free will.

We have choice and free will only within that which is man-sought *in a constant process of seeking.*

Wisdom too is man-sought and man-found. To seek philosophical wisdom is now something quite out of style; it does not fit into our world of know-how with its more-or-less precise knowledge. There is a mysterious imprecision to wisdom which defies fixed measurement. And because our technological faith is based upon ever more precise measurement, the imprecision of wisdom has become anathema.

And yet, when the recognition of the need for wisdom is disassociated from Man's intelligence, intelligence by itself leads us ever closer to terminal destruction.

Again and again, always, we return to the question? What is Man for? What is life for? Why life? This question — which has now assumed a life-importance which it never before had or could have had is, as it needs to be, the anchor of our inquiries within the multiple and expanding areas of inquiry.

ON 'GOOD INTENTIONS'
. . . the 'purity' of knowledge does not remain pure . . .

Because of our complexly interwoven world many 'good things,' good in their intentions, have turned out to be not good at all.

For instance: Several years ago I spoke with a United Nations official responsible for the rather broad application of DDT in certain parts of India with the aim of reducing childbed fever and infant mortality. His efforts were quite successful and he was rather proud—until he returned to the same area four years later and saw the many bloated bellies of the starving youngsters his work had helped survive. His anguish over what he had helped bring about was deeply distressing; and he asked, more of himself than of me: 'There was no evil intent; there was only good intent; yet look at the children. How could this be?' I asked him: 'If you had known the effects you now see of your DDT-application project four years ago, would you not have gone ahead with it?' And his haunted reply was: 'Heaven help me and these children. I would, I would.'

To reduce infant mortality without increasing the means to at least sustain the children is hardly a technological feat in which any of us can take pride.

We must be everlastingly alert—more now than before—to the dangers inherent in our actions even, and perhaps especially, when we believe them to be only for 'the good.' And it is not only in our actions that we need to become as far-sighted as possibly we can, but also—perhaps even more so—in our thoughts and ideas.

For instance: At one time in the not so distant past 'pure Science,' 'pure research,' was an expansion of human knowledge for the sake of knowledge. But for the past three decades and more we have noted again and again—and been witness to the fact—that the 'purity' of knowledge does not remain pure for long; it is quickly polluted with impurities precisely because the search itself for 'pure' knowledge rests on a base now become most tenuous. It is now based mainly upon the limpid belief that 'maybe we'll learn something useful.' But we can no longer afford such tenuousness. We ourselves have brought this about through our unquestioning acceptance of many things—and we've grown soft in our acceptances.

There were certain risks one could take at one time because there was sufficient 'absorptive capacity,' so to speak, in the world at large. But this absorptive quality is no longer present. It is as though the entire planet is now so saturated that certain risks within what is called 'research' are no longer risks but actual virulences which will not go away by themselves. Indeed, the concentration of hazard in our world—and not only bio-hazard—has never been more potent than it is now. And indeed too, we must be everlastingly alert to the virulences which may be present in our actions and ideas which may be transformed by others of effective power and bad intent.

The alertness to which I refer stems more from ethics than it does from surveillance. And a scientific 'ethic,' technological 'ethic,' human 'ethic,' cannot even begin to emerge—and to guide our enormous capabilities—without our attempting to understand as deeply as we can presently what 'the goodlife' means to us, and may mean to succeeding generations, whose lives we are affecting now in so very many gross and subtle ways.

MEDICAL ETHICS
. . . 'cost / benefit ratio' attitudes . . .

The University of California, in December 1976, issued a report edited by two professors of Ethics in its School of Medicine which should be of profound and immediate concern to us all, as well as to medical practitioners.

The report concluded that physicians should pull the plug of life-sustaining equipment that keeps severely defective newborn human beings alive; that the newborn should not be resuscitated when there is 'no *reasonable* expectation (my underlining) that the infant will ever be able to respond effectively and cognitively to human attention and caring or to engage in communication with others . . . Life-preserving intervention should be understood as doing harm to an infant who cannot survive infancy or who will live in intractable pain, or who cannot participate even minimally in human experience . . .' The report stated that it is *ethical* to stop therapy for an infant in order to provide care for another infant who has a much better chance of surviving and leading a normal life.

One of these professors of medical ethics is a former Jesuit priest who resigned his presidency of a Jesuit university in 1972 when he joined the faculty of UC's School of Medicine. The other professor, when the report was made public, was quoted as saying: 'It's a difficult area to discuss because it's very filled with emotions. We hope the report will help bring the issue out in the open.'

But I ask myself again and again, in trepidation and concern—and, yes, in anger too: 'What *is* the issue?????' Is it the medical determination of which infant is to live, and which is to die? Is the issue the question of deciding which infant is to receive the services of the sophisticated and costly medical equipment and which infant is not? Is the issue the question of *how* this decision is to be made? Is the issue the question of medical *triage* toward the newborn, of medical *practicality*? Or is the issue one of *medical* ethics being special and different within the overall concept of ethics?

There are so-called 'Right-to-die' laws in the USA aimed, theoretically, for the releasing from both pain *and* medical-costs of the senile and the terminally sick. Are such measures now to be imposed upon the newborn who are determined by medical practitioners to be terminal upon birth? The questions are many; and they are both frightening and agonising to us all because they indicate the direction increasingly being taken by the so-called 'cost/benefit ratio' attitudes within the medical profession. Of course medical technology is becoming ever more costly, and the profession is looking for some sort of rationale, some sort of 'ethical basis,' for its economic-determinism attitudes. Each of us, especially those of us with memories of the recent past still hauntingly alive within us, can visualise where all this can lead, and with accelerated haste.

The issue here, organic to each of the questions, is not one of *medical* ethics but of *ethics*.

And it is my contention here that the physician, *as physician*, is now incapable of ethical concepts but, at best, only of what is being called 'medical/ethical concepts'; that the physician as physician is so hooked up into machines which are both marvels of ingenuity and also very costly that his thinking, as a physician, is now inevitably technologicalised; that 'medical/ethical concepts' are themselves technology-governed. He may be more gifted as a physician than his predecessors, more gifted than Hippocrates or Maimonides — but not, thereby, more moral or more ethical. His patients may indeed benefit medically from his growing expertise and his skilful use of sophisticated equipment; but they and their offspring may well be harmed by his technologicalised morality and ethics.

To allocate the question of who shall live and who shall die to technological considerations — however well-intentioned — is to reduce the question to a cost-accounting *triage* level and to torsion essential moral/ethical principles without which we become less human and less humane. And the next inevitable descent here is frighteningly apparent: namely, that ethics may then be given consideration *only* within a cost/benefit framework, only if it is economically feasible to be concerned with ethics. And all this would not be limited only to medical ethics, but to other areas of human capability wherein the question of ethics needs to be ever-standing before us, especially now within our Man/Machine world of increasing medical-technological expertise, increasing populations — and decreasing resources.

ON TELLING PATIENTS 'THE TRUTH'
. . . a dangerous coarsening of the 'art' of Medicine . . .

A physician friend of mine — dedicated, competent, humane — completed the first chapter of a book he has long wanted to write on the subject of the responsibility of physicians to tell their patients 'the truth' of their medical diagnoses when they believe their patients have terminal or incurable conditions. He is persuasive in his reasons, and he draws many examples from his many years of practice. He believes there is an urgent need for his book because Medicine and its practitioners are becoming more technological and less humane, and the 'art' of Medicine is being lost to both physician and the patient.

In discussing his work he agreed that 'diagnostic truth,' if you will, is not the only 'medical truth' with which physicians need to be concerned—*as physicians.* 'Diagnostic truth' has now become only one segment affecting the physician's capacity to comprehend more of the overall complex of what could be called 'medical truth' and 'medical ethics' because these two are indeed closely interrelated. For instance: Three kidney-dialysis machines are available and four patients need them. What 'truth' does the physician use to arrive at his decision as to which of the four patients is to remain untreated and, thereby, drastically reduce his life-expectancy? Or does 'truth' not enter here because this question is, to the physician, isolated from 'truth'?

But physicians no longer can be isolated from the many nuances in contemporary Medicine because the medical complex has become interwoven with so many other things: with right-to-die attitudes and legislation; with abortion as a matter of political decision; with cost/benefit ratio business practices increasingly determining physicians' attitudes toward their patients. And what for instance, is happening to the physician's historic credo of belief in the sanctity of life when he is also concerned over population-pressures? And what is the dedicated physician's attitude, as a physician, to recombinant genetic engineering, and to so many other technological capabilities now available? And what of professors of 'Medical Ethics'—a relatively recent academic addition to some medical schools—who recommend that the infant born 'defective' should not be kept alive through special skill or techno-medical assistance?

At one time, even in the recent past, physicians were held in much higher esteem than they are at present, for which physicians themselves need to take the largest dose of blame. Too many have become mainly technicians and, in the process, have indeed lost the 'art' of Medicine; the 'art' of understanding the patient as a human being. And it is *a human being* to whom the physician will tell the truth regarding that human being's terminal or incurable condition.

The point here is that physicians, as physicians, have been much too silent and apparently unconcerned over many basic factors affecting human beings and have thereby earned much distrust.

They have isolated themselves within various segments of their professions; and when they are urged by one of their colleagues to tell 'the truth,' to what 'truth' can they refer? To the truth only of dying?

Can contemporary Medicine become increasingly more technological *as well as* increasingly more humane? This is a very important question truly because Medicine *will* become increasingly more technological. And if it cannot become more humane, the medical disregard of the human being as a human being, and not only as a patient, will also increase. And therein lies a dangerous coarsening of the 'art' of Medicine, and a dangerous corruption of 'truth' and ethics within the medical complex. The effect of this upon us all can indeed become incurable or terminal insofar as 'medical truth' and our trust in it is concerned.

MICROBIOLOGY AND 'A NEW SCIENTIFIC ETHIC'

. . . 'scientists' have been confused about their roles . . .

The sophisticated expertise within microbiology has now made it possible, through man-manipulated DNA and RNA factors, to graft a miscellany of qualities onto benign bacteria which can turn them 'by accident' into such virulent organisms for which there would be no human control, no antidote, and which could prove to be disastrous to life. The capability for this manipulation now exists in many laboratories in the USA and abroad.

The fear of this capability—and the fear of 'the accident'—is being discussed by some microbiologists, and by others in different areas of work, who are calling for what they term 'a new scientific ethic' to guide them in their investigations in order to avoid the disastrous possibility. It is quite a large step forward for scientists/ technicians to recognise the need for a new ethic for their work—

something quite generally ignored by the Atom Bomb people three decades ago. Yet, there is a threatening similarity between the older and the newer scientists/technicians.

Unhappily, it is not a 'scientific ethic' for which the microbiologists ask. Quite apparently, they are asking for new and stricter methods of *controlling* this beast which their expertise may release upon the world. And *control* is a far cry indeed from the need for a new ethic. It is not a 'new scientific ethic,' but a new *technological* ethic, a new procedure, which they euphemistically term 'a new scientific ethic.' And this confusion, this obfuscation, does not bode well for us all. Such obfuscation is becoming all too prevalent in our world of expanding expertise.

The term 'accident'—whether in microbiology or in nuclear proliferation—is much too pallid a word here; it is another euphemism, another substitution of a mild expression for something far more offensive. An 'accident' is an occurrence which, despite agony to the few, can be absorbed by the many. By definition, an accident is not something which can obliterate all life. Total erasure is not an accident; and neither is its threat.

For a long time now 'scientists,' or those who think of themselves as 'scientists,' have been confused about their roles and responsibilities. Many things are changed in our world now so indivisibly interrelated that, if things continue as they are, we may never again see 'Science as free inquiry.' The results of scientific research are now products in the sense that application is the goal, not 'free inquiry.' Indeed, we are increasingly realising that very little, if anything, in our world is now 'free.'

Instead of 'scientists' (of whom, parenthetically, there are so very few amongst the scientific/technological community) trying to grapple with some of the deeper questions which are at the bottom of their work, they are interested in getting more grants to do more 'research' with quite predetermined goals. And 'scientists' do not seem to see the difference—or care about it—even while they speak euphemistically about their work.

A 'new scientific ethic' is now so very essential, not only to those presently engaged in work which may affect mankind adversely, and not only to those who are now preparing themselves to enter this profession through which they will seek the goodlife for themselves and their children, but a new scientific ethic is now vital to us all precisely because our fabulous technological capability seems to be increasingly disassociating itself from the basic questions of human purpose and human striving within the complex of the 'ethical good' which we all, scientists and non-scientists, need to seek — everlastingly.

THE LIMITATIONS OF SCIENCE
. . . *no understanding through rationality alone . . .*

Science may soon reach its plateau of discovery, if it has not already done so.

I am not saying that there are no more principles of Science to be discovered. But these principles are within the area of philosophy evolving from Science as we have known it to be. These principles need to be sought in order to lend substance to the assumption that life will continue on Earth into the long foreseeable future.

During this parturition, the difficulty is that there are so many false and beguiling seductions: Easternisms, 'mysticisms,' primal screamings . . . their variations are legion, and legions follow one variation or another.

The human philosophical evolvement is a necessity if we assume that our life will continue on this planet. This does not imply a rejection of technology; it does imply that the dominance of technology over our lives will recede with the emergence of philosophical inquiry into being and essence of life, an inquiry stemming from Science as the evolving successor to Science as we have known Science to be: a human endeavour for the purpose of understanding the rational order of the Universe and its components. The individual human being is one of these components, and he is both rational and irrational. As individuals we also contain within us an a-rationality as one of the essential ingredients of being human and of being capable of further evolvement; and we can no longer understand our selves, much less the Universe, through rationality alone; the a-rational, this uniquely human gift, is also essential here.

The rational by itself is no longer sufficient to lend substance to our hopes and aspirations for continuation. Logical sequences by themselves are simply no longer substantial enough to lend *hopeful* meaning to our large capabilities. On the contrary, logical sequences by themselves now often add to our disquiet and despair. For instance: Earlier rational scientific inquiry into the basic structure of matter led to the logical probability that a nuclear explosive device could be made. And ever since The Bomb the basic policy-instrument for peaceful coexistence in our strained world has been based upon the belief that peace can be achieved only through equal fear equally shared. This policy is a rational outgrowth of proliferating nuclear power. A logical sequence of this policy is that we are to accept fear as the basic frame-of-reference for our continuation. And the resultant compressive moral coarsening continues, affecting many areas of our endeavours.

However, let us assume that no nuclear bomb had ever been constructed, and that the earlier rational scientific inquiry in this area was only for the sake of expanding our knowledge. It is logical that we would want to use the knowledge acquired in order to enhance life. Remaining unconcerned with the question of what life is for, the expedient result would have been nuclear proliferation for power-generation, and all the resultant hazards we now confront from radioactive waste-disposal and from the ever hovering threat that a nuclear bomb *could* be made by those who controlled the 'peaceful' generating plants. And we would be very much in the same hazardous situation in which we now find ourselves to be increasingly throughout the world.

The rational, by itself, is now quite apparently insufficient to lend guidance to our endeavours, and substance to our hopes. What then remains to us?

ON COSMOLOGICAL INQUIRY
. . . our present limited wisdom . . .

From our most primitive beginnings on Earth the human craft-expertise has been increasing in our attempts to acquire dominion over the planet, with the largest increase taking place during the past few decades. Our many recent 'scientific discoveries' have been essentially within the complex of sophisticated technology, of craft-expertise. Some of these discoveries are fabulous, as with some of the space-probes, and the DNA and RNA discoveries and their microbiological applications. Other equally fabulous discoveries may well emerge. That they are labelled as Science has proven to be constrictive to the expansion of scientific inquiry.

Since our total dependence upon the rational and the logical is now one of the factors leading us astray, what then could be the next qualitative evolutionary development within an expanded complex of Science? If we assume the continuation of human life, this development will be, of necessity, in our forthcoming philosophical evolvement into questions of Being and Existence, into questions of *What is Man for?* — not in terms of what he is to do, but in terms of what he can become — as our basic frame-of-reference emerging from all our past scientific-philosophical inquiry. Not to find answers, which may be quite beyond our human capability, but for the purpose of extending our present limited wisdom as far as possibly we can because of our increasing critical need to understand much more than we now do of where we are, and what our projectability may be — not especially in terms of abstractions such as 'What's beyond the beyond?' but in terms of our deepest and most intimate necessity for hope, this human ingredient presently in such short supply.

And this basic inquiry cannot occur external to cosmological inquiry because it involves the question of our own 'place' in all of Nature, in all of the Cosmos. It is a universal question embracing a universe, insofar as human intelligence and spirit can become capable of this embrace.

The a-rational now needs to become organically compounded into our evolving and expanding inquiry. And because the a-rational is more within the realm of Philosophy than of Science, the compounding of these two realms has now become essential and basic to our understanding of ourselves and of the Universe and the hope for our continuation.

The central reason for this is that 'Nature,' in its largest meaning, is, to our human perceptions, always rational, always governed (to anthropomorphise here) by its own reasons, so to speak. (Morality-immorality do not apply to Nature, only to Man.) Nature is systemic and logical in its own terms, some of which the human mind is gradually discovering and understanding. But we are also a-rational beings for whom the rational (or irrational) is not always sufficient for our own discovery and understanding. As individuals we are capable of many thoughts which we cannot understand through rationality alone, or through irrationality, both of which are human evaluations, human judgments. However, a human quality which is non-judgmental, missing here, hampers our understanding. To such thoughts we lend meaning to our inner selves only through an a-rationality we often cannot describe even to ourselves.

In many ways it is within the complex expansive area of the a-rational wherein we are often most alive to our selves.

_____

ON SEMINAL IDEA
. . . the multiple meanings to us of existence . . .

A seminal idea is that which Man creates, which Man-the-individual creates, and which leads us to, and exposes us as individuals to, the multiple Universes within us within which we discover and re-discover for ourselves the multiple meanings to us of existence.

But what *is* a seminal idea? Essentially it is a fundamental seed from which can emerge a complex genus of ideas affecting us in many near and distant ways.

Three seminal ideas, for example, are: Monotheism — the human relationship to Deity; Love — the human relationship to beyond-self; and the Man/Earth interrelationship.

Monotheism, which began as a religious faith, evolved into a belief in an *ordered* Universe capable of being comprehended by human beings. It was this belief in an ordered Universe which made possible the later attempts at rational explorations of the solar system, of our own galaxy, and of the Universe — and also of our own selves and our own place, as it were, in all the Universe. Man began to realise his own capabilities for explorations of the mysteries surrounding him, and of attempting to understand them in *human* terms.

These explorations were initially in terms of Idea, of theory stemming from belief in this Universe-order, as with the work of Copernicus, Kepler, Newton, Einstein. And because it proved to be an ordered Universe capable of human comprehension, their ideas concerning the Universe were later translatable into all sorts of ordered explorations, even unto Moon-landings and space-probes. Monotheism was the anchor to human explorations.

In early Monotheism, if the Heavenly bodies functioned at the whims of the gods, Heavenly order could indeed be irrational and incomprehensible and undependable to mere humans. Order, in its larger meaning of progression, could then exist on Earth itself only at the whims of the gods — and individual responsibility for such order on our life-giving planet would then be diluted. Floods and famines, for instance, would not be the results of human ignorance and avarice, even in part, because the gods were largely responsible.

With the passage of time during which its religious emphasis diminished, the seminal idea of Monotheism in its later ramifications lent a dependability to the Universe and a responsibility to Man as a conscious part of the Universe. This responsibility continues to grow as the human comprehension expands, and in a direct ratio one to the other.

Monotheism has proven to be perhaps mankind's greatest innovation in terms of seminal idea from which other ideas flowed and continue to flow. While seminal idea is mainly beneficent, it is not always totally so. In its basically religious aspect, Monotheism brought forth much agony to mankind throughout the ages.

The *idea* of love is another example of a seminal idea, in this sense: From the idea of love emerged Man's earliest concepts of intangibilities toward another life, especially within the complex spectrum of intangible needs and responsibilities. The *idea* of love extended Man's biological necessities and made it possible for the individual to see himself as being more than only a biological organism charged mainly with reproduction-responsibilities. Through the idea of love emerged the concept of self and beyond-self coexisting autonomously for mutual enrichment and evolvement. It is this concept which makes the existence of harmony a possibility—even a possibility—between and amongst people. And hope itself stems from the *idea* of love, however intangible both may be to an individual at any or many points of his life.

Perhaps one of the most important seminal ideas today is that of the Man/Earth interrelationship, and that Man's responsibility toward it cannot be relinquished to Deity in any form.

ON LANGUAGE
. . . one of the basic resources we possess . . .

Among our many 'ecological necessities,' the purification of language is as important as is the purification of water or air. Language is one of the basic resources we possess—not only for survival but also for evolvement. It is the instrument by which we interpret ourselves to ourselves: by which we can understand our fears and frustrations, and define our hopes and aspirations. We can recycle all of our products, but if we do not recycle and reclaim our use of language we will be lost even deeper than we now are in the badlands of our own making.

I am often asked what I mean when I speak of our 'organic need for re-definitions, for a re-defining of ourselves to ourselves.' My reply is usually based upon the following: We now call our technological skills 'Science.' When these skills are highly sophisticated we call them 'sophisticated science.' To me this means that we no longer know what Science is, was, could be, and needs to be. And soon we will have no need for what Science was, is, could be and should be. When we call all of our paintings 'art,' what do we mean by 'art'? And if we do not know or care to know, we will soon have no need to know.

If we designate our 'products' as 'processes' (as we do when we equate the accumulation of the products of our Man-Machine world with the processes of our search for the goodlife), there is soon no distinction needed between product and process. Even more to the point: it is the real meanings of 'science,' 'art,' 'process,' which we then diminish within ourselves. And what of words like 'freedom,' and 'liberty,' and 'honour,' which fall so discordantly upon our ears?

Surely we need to augment rather than to diminish ourselves; and we cannot augment or elevate ourselves without Idea, which has far more to do with 'science,' 'art,' 'process,' than with application/painting/product.

One of the coarsening aspects in our use of language has to do with the subjects with which we deal in words, and with our attitudes toward these subjects. Our use of language has lost dignity partly because *we* have lost dignity in our relationships with ourselves, with others, and with our habitat. Obscenity itself has lost its meaning when truly obscene words such as *overkill* and *kill-ratio* have not even been recognised as being obscene.

If we do not attempt to re-define ourselves to ourselves, we deny our own creative necessity and capability; we then copy our carbon-copy, so to speak, and present it as an original effort.

We are biological organisms capable of Idea. Idea is *natural* to this biological organism. When we deny our necessity for regeneration *from* Idea, we impose a biological limitation upon ourselves, upon our purpose, upon our past and our present and our future.

If, in our pressing current dilemmas, we manage to save ourselves, what are we saving ourselves for? If we can save ourselves through Idea, we have certainly saved ourselves *for* Idea . . . and to me this is only one aspect of our organic need to re-define ourselves to ourselves, in all the languages, spoken and unspoken, which we use.

ARE IDEALS 'IMPRACTICAL'?
. . . thinking for ourselves becomes less important . . .

Does 'practicality' mean that we are to discard ideas and ideals which cannot readily be embodied in some actuality, some activity? Does it mean that we will accept only those ideas which can be translated readily into something tangible? Does it mean that it is 'practical' for us *not* to have ideals, or to seek them? that ideals unrelated to direct action have become a hindrance in our problem-plagued world?

However, many ideas and ideals now labelled 'philosophical' have the greatest 'practicality' in our present world; indeed, it is now disastrously impractical to reject or dilute ideas and ideals — or to cease seeking them. It should be apparent as we look about us that our reservoir of Idea and Ideal is not full to overflowing; that indeed much of it has evaporated precisely through the heat of what is considered to be 'action,' leaving the residue murkily unclear.

Of course we are in a world desperately in need of 'action' on all sorts of levels. But we expend ourselves wastefully when our actions are random and haphazard, even when we intend them to be for the good.

The good itself cannot be identified except through idea and ideal.

We and the times are changing at an accelerated rate, and expediency is becoming ever more dominant in our public and private lives, and dangerously so in our thinking for ourselves. A backlog, indeed a growing logjam, of things large and small in need of doing presses in upon us from all sides. But randomly removing one log here and another there, however active the removal, will not unjam the mass but add to it. The basic need here, the critical need, is first to identify for ourselves, and then to remove if we can, the key logs causing the jamming.

This is difficult for us to do because we are subject more to persuasion than to our own thinking processes. As the skills of the persuaders increase they become more invasive, and our own thinking processes, our own evaluation processes, seem to shrink. And all commercialised persuasion is quite actually designed to lead us away from thought, from idea and ideal, and into some action— whether to purchase a particular brand of soap, a particular ideology, or a particular brand of instant awareness and enlightenment. Thinking for ourselves becomes less important the more we succumb to persuasion, especially commercialised persuasion, because we then believe that we are getting something tangible and *practical* for our payments.

Those who consider 'philosophical ideas' to be 'impractical' in a world of growing practicality seek to deal with problems, and with their concepts and quests for the goodlife, in tangible mechanistic terms which lend themselves readily to rationalisation, manipulation and public persuasion.

Idea and Ideal now have the highest practicality in our world. When we demean them because we consider them to be impractical, we relinquish our responsibility to think and become the persuaded—first to one fad, then to another, then to still another. And we expend our substance on the passing fads which, should we begin to think for ourselves, leave us with a feeling of emptiness and loss.

If we do not give utmost personal value to ideas and ideals we soon lose our needs, and then our abilities, to think for ourselves.

ON IMPATIENT ACTIVISTS
. . . 'instant everything . . .'

Waves of activism have swept across the campuses of America and other parts of the world from time to time, and then receded into placidity. They were energy-generating; occasionally they were cleansing; most often they expended themselves on unyielding shores. In retrospect they accomplished only little in their stated attempts to modify the status quo of their educational structures, societal structures, or of themselves. Their accomplishments—some of which were indeed laudable—were not in proportion to their activism.

When activism is based on inadequate knowledge and tenuous idea, it is fed by turbulent emotions; and these emotions, when they peak, are usually destructive to whatever Cause the impatient activists initially addressed themselves, even if they did so with high purpose. Also, emotional roilings are indeed exhaustive to the participants.

When based upon idea, however, and nourished by expanding knowledge organic to that base—and, furthermore, by patience— activism can be effective.

One of the characteristics of our age (not only among young people) is a growing impatience with status quo and with our selves. In spite of numerous 'meditationists,' this is an age of 'instant everything,' with little time taken for reflection. This is not so much because we magnify the moment, but because our loss of faith in tomorrow, in *later,* leaves us with nothing but the *now.* And when Idea requires of us *now* a commitment to *later,* we become impatient.

Because our knowledge about so many things (perhaps I should say, information about many things) has increased at a much greater rate than our wisdom, the very idea of wisdom—which takes so much longer—seems to have become faded and non-essential.

Wisdom stems in part from Idea and the Ideal, as viewed within one's time—and these indeed do evolve and are not static. When idea and the ideal have no *utility* for us in the present, the question of wisdom becomes meaningless, often anathema, and even a hindrance to us and to our relationship with others. We are then left with lethargy, or with instant, impatient activism as the major pursuit worthy of our capabilities and efforts.

Imagine what our world might be if our active states of being were based upon our quests for wisdom—ongoing quests. Our perceptions of *now* would change, as would our impatient activism within the *now.* Our view of ourselves, of later time, of hope itself, would deepen and sharpen. Our activism, no longer powered by waves of turbulent emotion, no longer roiled, would be many times more effective. And our quest for wisdom, within activism, would lend meaning to endeavours that are worthy of our committed efforts and expanding capabilities.

The search for idea, ideal, wisdom, is a basic need of human beings; for lack of better words, it is our evolutionary 'destiny.' To seek only for what we can do with our clever brains and hands renders our destiny purely technological, and its end foreseen.

But if it is *what we may become,* idea, ideal, wisdom, then mean something special — indeed unique — to us.

PUZZLING PHILOSOPHIES
. . . and the desperate need . . .

For a long time I've puzzled over the question: Why is it that despite space-probes and moon-walks, radio telescopes and electron microscopes, despite massive data-piles and computerised communication and fabulous and often breath-taking technology, despite broader information more broadly disseminated than ever before, despite astonishing medical/behavioural projects and investigations, despite-despite-despite . . . why, with all these inventions and extensions, have we come up with no valid philosophy, no new way of viewing, to instruct and guide us in our changed, frustrating, sometimes exhilarating, and always perilous lives. During the past quarter-century, most of the technological world has jettisoned its old philosophies. Why, then, no new?

One reason may be this:

Philosophies of the past sought to *explain* us to ourselves through the imposition of external idea evolved through external 'philosophical perspectives' in terms of what we *are* (or appear to be), and never in terms of what we may become — especially, not in terms of our human biological responsibility to our selves and to the planet Earth on which we live. Because philosophy has always been involved with the non-biological, Man has been regarded from a framework removed from the biological. Our spiritual component was external to our biological being.

In a direct sense the philosophical, the *actual* question of what we are, and what we are here for, is an evolving one. Our human capability, and incapability, cannot be amputated from our biological being. We are anchored in it. But an anchor fulfills its purpose only when it permits relative freedom to the vessel to which it is tied. If the vessel is tied so rigidly to the anchor that no movement is possible, then winds and tides can shatter it even while the now useless anchor remains imbedded.

All biological organisms have evolved. Sometimes they have devolved. The attempt of Man-the-Individual to transcend, to reach beyond his biological limitation is a continuing biological *and* philosophical process. When the attempt is fully and forcefully made, the process is evolutionary and can be supra-evolutionary. When no attempt is made, the process falters and becomes devolutionary. Frequently we now find ourselves between peak and trough, in a Limbo of non-commitment.

We have always been more in the trough than on the peak. Many now trying to climb from the trough of biological limitation, ascend a little way, then rope ourselves to lesser peaks in order not to fall into deeper troughs. It is so much harder to climb than to slide, even when we know the backslide may accelerate into a rubble-trailing fall.

To all of us the passage of time should bring an enriching process of enlightenment, of discovery and, especially, of re-discovery of our inner autonomy. Instead, time's passage so often generates such fatigue in us that even the thought of trying to climb is depressing.

The search for, the climb toward, an answer to what we humans really are, and what we are here *for,* is critical. We are in desperate need of a new philosophy which takes into organic consideration our kinship with all of life, with all of the planet — and, as human beings, with our largely unexplored capabilities to evolve, and, especially, with our *uniquely* human and humane responsibilities.

ON 'THE GOLDEN AGE OF MAN'
. . . *we could be within its beginnings* . . .

Many say, and have said, that mankind is now living within 'the last days of the Golden Age of Man.' In a material sense, in a resources-consumption sense, this is probably so. There are no more easily arable acres remaining on our planet, even as Earth's population continues to proliferate. There is virtually no virgin water for human consumption remaining throughout this continent, and we are reduced to using processed and re-processed water, and at increasing energy-costs. The examples are so very numerous, and we are each affected by them.

In many material ways we are indeed within what has been called 'the last days of the Golden Age of Man,' perhaps now more gilded than golden.

However, in a non-material sense we could be, if we so truly wished, within the beginnings of a new Golden Age—an age wherein more and more of us are beginning to question our selves in terms of human purpose, of what life is for, of what Man is for, of what *we* are for, within the context of Idea. And Idea not limited to the question of what Man *is*, but with current knowledge and expanded vision to see before us what Man may become. It would be an awakening in its simplest and most profound meanings.

If this could be so, as it needs to be, our beneficent effects even upon the materiality of mankind and the planet would be simply enormous. We would see ourselves both as we are and as we need to be; at the very least, as we need to try to be.

But this cannot come about, in my view, through manipulations of material resources, whether through the Committee of Rome studies or the Net Energy studies now becoming popular—both are playing on the same game-board with mechanised rules and equations, and with human beings as mechanised pawns. Increasingly more people throughout the world are at least beginning to realise that to continue along present paths leads mankind backward toward the primordial ooze.

We are now at a point which resembles the final hours or days during which one finally recognises one's past errors and divergences, and one says in lamentation and despair: 'If only, if only

. . .' The difference here is that an individual may indeed be at this point within his final days. But unless something man-made horrendously bad erases all life from the planet, mankind is not within its final days. And, by the definition of mankind, many of the individuals composing mankind also are not.

I believe that mankind now possesses for the first time a fantastic opportunity to begin to understand something of human 'destiny,' if you will, which mankind never before possessed — not during the times of Hammurabi, of Socrates, of the religious leaders East and West, of Einstein.

It is an opportunity, more broadly based than ever before in history, emerging out of the past and present debris of our own making, and which has been decaying in a compost-pile for many years. Unlike the nuclear-pile fertilising poisonous weeds, this compost-pile can now be used to fertilise, not a Garden containing the Biblical Two, but a Garden of Earth containing thousands of millions.

If this could be so, as indeed it needs to be, our beneficent effects upon our selves and all succeeding generations upon our planet will indeed begin to fulfill the promise of human 'destiny,' so intimately interwoven with our continued evolvement throughout all remaining generations.

THE MARS-LANDER
. . . contemplating our own lush but troubled Earth . . .

The Mars-lander in July 1976 with its functioning miniaturised scanners and laboratories remains a magnificent technological achievement — a wizardry — which offers us all still another opportunity to grasp the significance of our place in all of Nature; an opportunity, yet fraught with the hazard of misinterpretation.

The wondrously skilled scientists/technicians responsible for this first effective Mars-landing will now seek other expansive projects based upon the success of this one, and in the heat of their exuberance they may well believe that Man is no longer Earth-bound — that Man's destiny is in the ever deeper explorations into space. And who can fault them?

In my view the Mars-landing demonstrates that we are more Earth-bound than ever and that we need to find magnificence in *that* realisation.

The human destiny is not, in my view, to explore other planets in our and other solar systems. Our destiny is to *interpret* cosmo-*graphic* explorations for the purpose of our own cosmological evolvement which itself embraces the unique nature of uniqueness itself. It is not a question of what we can *do* but of what we can *become.* The Mars-landing adds another ingredient to bolster our technological faith and our technological spirit — a rather curious juxtaposition of words. Yet the interpretation of the implications of the Mars-lander is not necessarily within the province of the many technological people who have done a grand job of cosmo-graphic work. We now need interpretations — cosmological inter-pretations, if you will — equally magnificent; and these will surely take time, and also contemplation, to emerge.

The views of Mars which we see only in photographs — strange views indeed, familiar but strange — provide us an opportunity of contemplating our own lush but troubled Earth and our inescap-able interrelationship with it.

While everything we experience is to us experiential, so to speak, there is a difference between the directly experiential and the experiential at a once-remove. In our highly visual and instru-mentally communicative world this difference is deeply significant because it affects our intimate responses to many things, including experience. For instance: 'Being there' has a dimension of reality which is missing in our viewing a photograph or a 'picture' of experience, so to speak. Yet so much of the great, moving and indeed awful realities of the past thirty years have come to us through such pictures; in newspapers, magazines, and of course television. This once-removal has made many of these events some-thing apart from us so that our own 'reality' stemming from such experience is also at a once-remove. The focus of distant things does not reach our retina, so to speak.

Through such once-removal we have become conditioned to accept many unpalatable things so long as they don't impinge upon us directly. For example: We may never have seen a starving child, yet hunger is a virulence which exists *now* and which can overtake the world, as it will if we do not recognise its realities to us *now*. Despite all the photographs presented of starving children, they are at a once-remove from us and our consciousness. How can we grasp their implications, direct implications, to us?

The Mars-lander is indeed experiential to us, but at a once-remove; the sights and sounds of explanation are all at a once-remove, experientially once-removed from us, as so many of our experiences have become. And yet, there *is* a mystery and grandeur to this magnificent technological achievement. And the question rises before us in many implications: Does Mars more readily awaken our sense of mystery than Earth? Is our capability for the contemplation of mystery and grandeur — and uniqueness too — to be confined only to that which we experience indirectly through our magnificent devices? Is our capability for the contemplation of mystery and grandeur and uniqueness to be confined only to that which is at a once-remove from us? Is such contemplation possible for us only when we have magnificent devices?

What a cosmic mockery this limitation makes of the Mars-landing achievement and its wizardry.

The astounding photographs from Mars indeed have this once-remove quality of unreality; and the mystery and grandeur of this event in terms of our relationship to our Earth do not — not yet — reach the retina of our soul, so to speak. And they cannot reach us in terms of our own interpretation so long as we ourselves remain unreachable to our own contemplation of mystery and grandeur and uniqueness — which is a language of the spirit that is not at all in competition with, or in rejection of, the language of the machine, so to speak.

It is in the nature of human destiny that the language of the machine, however sophisticated, can be at best only crude — while the interpretive expansive language of the spirit can indeed soar.

'LIVING WITH NATURE'

. . . our everlasting need to live harmoniously with Nature . . .

In Thoreau's time the call to 'live with Nature' had a different meaning than it does today, with 220-million Americans peopling the continent and with 4,000-million individuals blanketing the planet. To 'live with Nature' means something qualitatively different now, and we need to be aware of the difference and its many significances to us. Thoreau, born in 1817, could during the 45-years of his life, enter Nature, so to speak, enter the wild, by going to Walden Pond—a relatively simple entry. When he did so he rejected the nearby town and its amenities, and he could supply most of his needs quite readily from Nature—from what was available to him in his somewhat tamed wilderness. He deliberately simplified his needs so that he could be as independent of the town as was possible for him; and at that time in emerging America it was relatively simple to simplify one's needs, especially if one felt a sense of 'higher purpose,' so to speak, as Thoreau surely did. Today simplification of needs, of the simple needs of existence, would probably seem quite unsimple to Thoreau.

No matter how much one simplifies one's life today, to 'live with Nature' is rather complex, if by 'Nature' is meant living in the wilderness and supplying all of one's needs from the wilderness while, simultaneously, not imposing our contaminations upon the wilderness.

The point here is this: The *idea* of 'living with Nature,' Nature in its all-embracing meaning, and not only in its meaning of wilderness, has an everlasting inescapable reality to it no matter how changed the actuality may be—or may become. We are all part of Nature and never apart from it. One actuality is that there are simply too many people, and the numbers are increasing. But this actuality, or any conceivable actuality, does not invalidate our everlasting need to live harmoniously with Nature. Why then is this need not one of our guiding principles?

Our basic misguidances here are twofold, in my view: One is the belief that we can ultimately 'control' Nature; that we are so blessedly clever that we can move rivers from the Yukon, for instance, and water the deserts of the hemisphere—and what changes this would bring to the upper latitudes, and to the more southern ones as well, are given little consideration. The other simultaneous mistake, in my view, is the belief that we can, if we so wished, *return* to Walden Pond.

Both beliefs are basic mistakes leading us astray. We need to understand where we are *now,* and what the multiple things are which we need to begin doing *now* in order for us to continue to live within Nature—not as Nature is now as a result of our contaminations, but as Nature needs to be, through our purifications, if life is to continue. We need both to conserve and to purify, simultaneously, our life-giving resources. But we need to realise, again simultaneously, that such conservation and simplification and purification *is not a return* to earlier times; it is not a return at all, but a way of present and future life. To think of it as a return is to believe that we can escape the present, which we cannot do. But we can modify the present way-of-life and, thereby, help conserve the succeeding way-of-life. The differences here are quite significant and very much in need of understanding. It isn't a matter of giving up automatic washers, for instance, so much as of conserving water and fuel. An oversimplification? Perhaps. Well, look about you and you will surely find many of your own examples.

No, we cannot return; yet we should never forget Walden Pond because we should never forget how things were: the pure waters and also the smallpox; the government non-interference and also the near-universal illiteracy; the grand open spaces of the country and also the open sewers of the cities; Thoreau and the older Emerson who outlived him by twenty years, and also the New England slave-traders . . . No, we should never forget 'Nature' as it was then—little understood but accepted—and 'Nature' as it is now, more understood and, alas, less accepted.

ON LAND
. . . we cannot replace the irreplaceable . . .

An acre contains 43,560-sq-ft or 4,047-sq-metres. Imagine one food-yielding acre of our planet—which is an area smaller in size than the paved parking lot of a large supermarket. Imagine, too, that in our projections and expectations *that* given one acre is expected to yield food for a number of years: 5-years, 100-years, 10,000-years. (10,000 years is quite a short time in many ways; yet it is about equal in years to what we know of Man in his present culture.)

How could a given acre of land be expected to yield food for that long? Isn't even the expectation astonishing? Is it graspable? Yet, if you think on it even briefly, that is surely our expectation. Virtually by definition we cannot replace the irreplaceable, and Earth for us *is* irreplaceable. That given one acre, to be productive, would need continuous restoration, over and over and over again—a duty willingly passed along through many generations of mankind.

But it is not only the land which needs to be preserved. Actually, the land cannot be preserved at all without our also preserving the *attitudes* toward preservation which need to be fostered and passed through generations as one of mankind's most precious gifts for which there is no synthetic substitute.

Can we develop and encourage such attitudes toward preservation, even at this somewhat late date? Indeed we can, even as we must.

For instance: So many of the nearly 3,000 colleges in the USA are situated where there is land available for cultivation. The colleges serve an enormous quantity of food to their students and faculty. Why can't the colleges, as a matter of course, attempt to grow much of the food that they consume and that is purchased at increasingly higher prices? I'm not referring to Agricultural Colleges with their test-plot gardens; neither am I referring to food-growing projects in order to train students to be small-acreage farmers. I *am* referring to the fact that every student needs to take some required courses. Let one of those courses be in tending the food-yielding acres so that students and faculty, and administrators too, will be aware—consciously and in their own energy and time expenditures—of their organic connection, year after year after year, with the food-yielding acre, and with its continuous need for restoration.

(Parenthetically, isn't it strange and pointed that in the USA the most nearly self-contained units in terms of food, each housing thousands of people, are the prisons of the country, with their prison farms and bakeries?)

Beginning in the hundreds of thousands of grade schools in this country and abroad, and continuing through the colleges and universities, let there be Land Education courses wherever possible, in addition to Physical Education courses.

The twelve or sixteen years of a student's life spent within educational systems could offer a continuum of awareness toward the land, toward the food-producing acre, and toward Earth itself. And the concept and actuality of continuous restoration and preservation could indeed become organic to millions of young people—and to their elders who have assumed responsibility for their education and growth.

WE ARE NOT AT GROUND ZERO
. . . measurable material impact has indeed been made . . .

The River Thames, as it passes through London, is now cleaner than it has been since Queen Victoria's reign. The people, and the authorities, through awareness and necessity, finally did something about the unacceptable pollution—and the River responded.

Just imagine if there had been no public awareness concerning the deteriorating environment and waterways and oceans, no Clean Air Act, no Environmental Protection Agency, and equivalent Acts and Agencies in other countries, no growing awareness regarding proliferating populations. Just imagine if throughout the world we had continued to maintain the attitudes of only a few years ago. We still have a deteriorating environment, deteriorating water-quality, and population-increases. But can one imagine what these would have been by now without those awarenesses?

No, we are not starting from Ground Zero even though the problems remain and have grown larger. These problems would have been grotesquely huge by now, and their rate of acceleration would have been so much larger. This rate is too large as it is, but it need not be immobilising. The proof of this is in the fact that some measurable material impact has indeed been made. Population-increases throughout the world, large as they are, would have been larger by some 75-million if we had continued to maintain the rates-of-increase of a decade ago. The environment, endangered as it is, would have been far more so had we not had a change in our attitudes. The change is not yet deep enough because the environment is in constant threat—probably even more so now than a year ago due to all sorts of energy/environment trade-off attitudes re-emerging in this country and in other industrialised countries.

Nevertheless, we are not at Ground Zero, and we can indeed take strength, if not solace, from this. And we need this strength because we are in an age of shortages—many of which are real, many of which are contrived. Even those contrived will become real tomorrow or the day after, next year or the year after, since all material resources, by their very nature, do reach points of depletion and exhaustion. And the strength referred to here needs to be applied to our steadfast realisation of the many strictures of limitations we do confront—and not to become immobilised by them, despite attempts to foist upon us numerous crises in understanding and awareness, qualities in short supply.

And precisely because we are at present, quite demonstrably, not at Ground Zero, these are shortages about which we *can* do something—indeed many things both quantitative in terms of resources, and qualitative in terms of our human and humane selves.

THE MOON AND MARS LANDINGS
. . . yet the human spirit falters . . .

In July 1969 Man first set foot upon the Moon in a magnificent feat of technological wizardry, termed by the then President of the USA as 'the greatest event since The Creation.' Even at the moment of the landing on the Moon the killing on Earth continued to be pursued with all the technological expertise the military could command; and the killing continued in Vietnam and elsewhere for days and months and years. What did mankind learn from the Moon-landing and the Earth-killing? What did the power controllers learn? The swords have not been turned into ploughshares; and Damocles' own Sword swings ever-lower just above us, adding its own hisses to our age of fear and near panic.

Seven years ago to the day of the first human landing on the Moon, only a quarter-million miles away, an utterly remarkable man-made device landed effectively on Mars, 200-million miles from us. And on that day too the killing continued in the Near East and elsewhere. What is the nature of 'magnificence' in this context. Will we ever change? Will we ever learn?

We were intrigued, even fascinated, by the Moon-landing; we were intrigued, even fascinated, by the Mars-lander. If these are only passing fascinations, all the technological wizardry is only a spatial Disneyland for which we have paid heavy entrance-fees.

It is the genius of Man-the-Individual that he is capable of being astonished — not of astonishing another, a spectator, but of being himself astonished — and to retain this capability throughout his life. I doubt that many people contain this genius for very long; events leach it from most of us permanently, and from all of us from time to time of varying spans. Yet without this capability for astonishment — so very different from entertainment or amusement — individual creativity itself falters, hesitates, and is then directed into other less deep channels.

The fabulously huge varieties and — that curious word in this context — 'subsets' of life on Earth, for instance, are astonishing. What sort of person has an ongoing, a relatively ongoing, astonishment over this? It is not at all an idle question. To retain the capability of being astonished is, at the very least, vital to self-evolvement and creativity, and to an intimate sense of one's own cosmological awareness as distinct from cosmographical knowledge. Knowledge, of itself, will not 'make us free' to resolve our man-made dilemmas. Indeed, knowledge unrelated to the deep-rooted need to comprehend our own place in all of Nature, to understand what we are for, is now more often than not a misdirection of our capabilities and our needs. Knowledge of itself will not make us change *our* selves, and for the better. Yet this change is surely one of our most basic needs. If we believe this to be impossible to us we forfeit much of ourselves and the inescapable Man/Earth interconnectedness.

During the seven years between the Moon and Mars landings much knowledge has been added to our arsenal—yet the human spirit falters. I doubt that any technological feats in space or on Earth can levitate the human spirit, which can rise only from within each of us. And this does not come easily—not to you, not to me, not to anyone of awareness and concern; not to anyone who ongoingly knows and feels the utterly basic difference between what we are, what we may have been and, perhaps in hope, what we may yet become—in ascent and not descent.

Will we, or can we even learn from the Moon or Mars landings so long as we do not expand and deepen our own awarenesses and comprehensions of Earth and of the Man/Earth interrelationship? We take our limitations with us—and our expansions too.

OUR WONDROUS PLANET
. . . a fragile Earth giving life to us . . .

Everything we know of our solar system bespeaks of the wonders of our planet. Earth *is* our only habitat of which we know, and also the only habitat of birds and trees, of earthworms and fishes; of human beings capable of wonderment, thoughtful creativity and deliberate destruction.

Consider the wonder of the seed, plant and human; of its growth and maturity, and its reseeding. The wonder of so many different languages; of how much we know and how little we know. Nowhere else in our solar system is there living land like ours; land upon which we live and create and recreate, land upon which we *can* walk erect; land which, with our joined efforts, brings forth harvests to nurture us.

The streams and the seas—in each drop of their waters are miracles for us to behold; and in each spoonful of soil a lifelong study.

The diversity of our Earth is such that no one person can ever know all its places, all its grandeur. There is so much to appreciate every morning upon awakening, every night before recuperative sleep, every hour as we look about us and actually see with our outer and inner vision.

Once it was The Garden for two of us, and for the serpent as well; it is now the garden for 4,000-million of us, and also for many serpents. There are many diversities within each of the 4,000-million of us, for we are human beings and neither angels nor devils; and many diversities within the serpents as well, for many of them are of our own making, fanged with our own man-made poisons.

Within each of us are wondrous diversities of emotions and responses throughout all our individual ages, in our agonies and exhilarations, our actualities and imaginations, for we are complex human beings upon a living Earth which needs all of life. We are the continuum of all human existence upon a fragile Earth giving life to us and to all other things and beings. Neither angels nor devils exist upon our Earth; if they have existence it is within us.

Yes, we stand upon the shoulders of all the past, Einstein's as well as Hitler's—for we are the continuum. Einstein and Hitler—neither angel nor devil, but human; and also of our Earth.

The deepest deprivation is the loss of wonder; and the singular sin of any age is the deliberate destruction of wonder.

Those who fang our serpents are the planters of the weeds of decay; and we—all of us—are the captive harvesters. And yet, and yet—need we *be* captives?

ON JEREMIADS AND THE FUTURE
. . . an attempt to escape both present and future . . .

It is quite easy to hurl jeremiads or quiet-toned lamentations that we are now past the Golden Age of Man and that the future is an ever-tightening downward spiral.

Such projections can be made with earnest persuasiveness and with some validity. But to what avail? To read the entrails of sheep-like beings? To be forewarned of future and thereby fore-armed against descent?

But we live in a world of logarithmic change wherein the *now* has become so magnified to us that the future has little personal meaning to too many of us. Perhaps we are so afraid of the future that we are reluctant to think about it for ourselves. And the fear permeates us now, in the present. To quieten the fear we involve ourselves in all sorts of active immediacies so that increasingly we live only for the moment. Even to Western meditationists meditation is an activity for the moment. We follow one costly fad promising salvation of some personal easement, and then another immediate costly fad when the earlier one defaults, and then still another. We are hurried and harried in an attempt to escape both present and future. But the present is inescapable, as is the future.

Yes, the future does appear to be bleak in many ways, especially in material ways. It is a bleakness brought on by the present and the recent past for which we are accountable. To continue with our present profligacies will surely make the future even more bleak—and it is this fact which is so very difficult for us to accept as a fact of our present lives. We give this fact some lip-service upon occasion, but we do not seem to absorb it into our very beings. Does the American motorist, for instance, truly accept the reality of the limitation of fossil fuels, of gasoline at the pump? Does he accept the concept of material limitations, much less the actuality of such limitation—of Earth's arable acres? of the planet's breathable atmosphere, of global water-supplies and availabilities?

If he could make such acceptances *in the present,* and transmit them to his children as his parental and human responsibility, he would realise that he cannot create his life, and help them create theirs, out of material things only or even mainly. He may then look upon the future with more challenge to his ingenuity and resiliency than with fear.

To be told by whatever experts what the material future will be for him is one thing. But to accept such predictions as inevitable determiners of the quality-of-life for him and his progeny is quite something else. In terms of the material future we are surely past the age of global material affluence. In terms of the non-material future we may well be at quite another beginning. But we have become so soft in our affluence that we may indeed become temporarily immobilised when the crutch — externally gilded but internally made of baser metal — collapses even as we lean upon it.

It is not the future against which we need to be forewarned. It is against the softening processes of the present which should demand our attention and responsibility.

Consider the reality that our expectations for decades, and still ongoing, were stimulated and directed toward incremental materialities and not toward attempts at deeper understanding of the human dilemma — and the human glory. Capable of being nearer to God than the Angels within the context of human creation, we construct the fabric of our lives out of the glittering cosmetical and only so very rarely do we seek the elusive cosmological. And yet, it is becoming increasingly evident that whatever Man is for, he is surely not for the purpose of accumulating material things at the expense of others and of this life-giving planet. Whatever Man is for he is surely not for rapacity and avarice.

While the future may be materially bleaker than now, the human enrichment does not lie only, or even mainly, within the material sector. *It never did.* Perhaps we are now finally being forced to recognise this ongoing reality and its many implications to us now, and for the future.

ASTRO-BEDAZZLERS
. . . *Earth only as a launching pad* . . .

The growing public interest in popularised astronomy and cosmography should give us all a clearer view of our own Earth and its astonishing preciousness. There is today much talk of the probability of life on other planets, of the marvels of space-cities, of the grandeurs of our technological capabilities to send jewel-like probes to distant places—but the connection of all this with our own planet seems tenuous, flimsy. It is not as though the popularisers talk of Earth only as a launching-pad; but they do talk of it as though it were a way-station, as something temporary, as something to leave, as something which is not habitat. They talk eloquently of the largeness of the Cosmos but they approach it with miniaturised smallness toward Earth and its life, including human life.

The point here is this: All life, as we know life to be, is singular—this is a biological fact. When the hive is destroyed, for instance, the bees may die; and even if their deaths are group-deaths, it is death within the group of individual bees. Life is singular to the organism, even though every organism is interrelated with everything else.

All matter is subject to certain laws, by definition, which we may through increasing knowledge and insight discover. All matter is subject to chemical/physical laws; and the point of qualitative change from physics to chemistry or chemistry to physics is frequently obscure. Only very rarely does chemistry change qualitatively into biology, even more rarely does physics change so. Within biology the organism does follow certain chemical and physical laws. In Man, for instance, chemical laws abound, as do physical laws pertaining to structure and mass. Yet within Man it is the biological factors which dominate in terms of response.

Life, however interconnected, is indeed singular to the organism; chemistry is not singular, neither is physics. It is this singularity of response, reaching its peak in Man's capability for thought, which attempts to evolve a cosmological view. Earlier terracentric and helio-centric belief were discarded as knowledge of the Cosmos increased, and astronomers began to realise that neither Earth nor Sun were the centre of the Universe. Later astronomers began to seek a Homocentric belief in Cosmology—a belief that Man, through his capability for thought, lent a centre, so to speak, to the Universe. Contemporary astronomers and cosmologists seek to reject this Homocentric belief because of the chemical/physical dominance in the Universe.

And yet, quite apparently, they do not lend proper substance to the nature of biology, to the singularity of response within biology, and to the nature of human thought. And it is this singularity of thought, reaching its peak in Man, which attempts to evolve a Cosmological view. But it is an unavoidable and curiously *biological* view of a Cosmos essentially not biological. Simply attributing biological qualities to matter does not make it life-like, however enticing such attributions may be.

Now then, chemistry/physics cannot be compared to biology. We *discover,* as observers, chemical and physical laws; it is we who learn the validity of these laws. Once discovered they remain valid throughout the total spectrum. When we, through new knowledge and insight, discover that an earlier law was not so, it was also not so through the total spectrum. But biology is constantly changing, and only very few fixed laws can be established.

When the ever-changing biology-in-man seeks to establish Cosmological theory he is inevitably using his changing biology to evolve a theory concerning unchanging chemistry and physics. And this is the basis for the human Cosmological dilemma. It is an historic dilemma and it will be an ever present one precisely because Man cannot remove himself from his biological self. This does not reject the probability of life on other planets of distant galaxies; and this does not imply that we can only have, inevitably, a Homocentric view of the Cosmos and, thereby as is now happening with popularity, endow life to chemical/physical substances in the Universe. Indeed, to do so may be bedazzling, especially to young people who may be looking for some sort of extraterrestrial meaning. But to do so minimises human life, and is corruptive of the Man/Earth interrelationship.

This historic dilemma, stemming from our own biological inevitability and responsibility, does mean that we, as living beings on a life-giving planet, cannot ever disregard human life and thought in any Cosmological theory we may evolve through our singularity and our gifts.

PLANNING AND EDUCATION
. . . *a process of education as well as activism* . . .

City, county, regional, state and national planning is a relatively recent profession in the USA, and most professional planners in the country have little educational/academic background in this complex area. The elected officials controlling planners usually have *no* educational background in this subject—something they surely need. Of course the factor of re-election seems to be foremost in the minds of elected officials, which is not a bad thing so long as they themselves are subject to an informed and alert electorate.

How far ahead should professional planners reasonably be expected to plan? And what could be the least common denominator in planning?

Basic to all planning is the obvious question: Planning for what? for what purpose? To help bring forth 'orderly growth,' whatever that means? to help increase the revenue tax-base for the community? to help a citizenry achieve a goodlife, whatever that means? Of course much depends upon the professional planner's job. Nevertheless, it surely would seem that all planning needs to be incremental: that is, short-term, medium-term, long-term. Short-term planning is nearly always reactive: a crisis in water or fuel, for instance, would bring forth certain reactions from planners. But even here the long-term effects of crisis should be used for educational purposes within planning. Medium-term planning may also be reactive to a crisis already upon the horizon but not yet impinging upon people. Here too the long-term effects need to be part of the education of the populace, elected officials, and planners. It is usually in the medium-term that professional planners may be able to contribute most effectively to the education of the populace—and themselves. This applies to planning from local to world-embracing levels. The long-term? This may seem far too distant to the populace, including planners and officials, for it to have much educational effect upon them.

I believe that all planning needs to be a process of both education as well as activism. In my view all planning needs to be one of the instruments for deepening the awareness of people (planners included) of the Man/Earth interrelationship; awareness of the limitations of all resources; awareness of the *necessity* to the individual and to all societal structures of intangible resources, such as hope, trust, responsibility to future and so on.

At one time I suggested to the Chief Planner of an affluent county that he and members of his staff arrange a series of evening seminars—*not* project-oriented, but on the overall subject of planning. He thought the idea a good one, but unworkable. His objections were essentially two-fold: His Supervisors, he thought, may not like the idea of such seminars being organised and attended by county-employees since the seminars were not oriented to any particular project under county consideration; and, he said, 'the planners were so busy during the week that asking them to give up an evening a week, without pay, would be asking too much of them . . .'

And yet, the least common denominator of all planning is, to me, the educational value to both the planners and the planned-for. And while long-term planning must never be avoided, all short-and-medium-term planning should be within the framework of long-term planning.

The USA has recently celebrated its Bicentennial; and I should think that long-term planning should extend for at least another 200-years. Medium-term planning should extend until at least the end of this century. And short-term planning, depending as it does upon crisis arrived, is always reactive, and not planning at all. And much planning offered by the professionals in this complex area is, alas, only reactive.

ON DE-NOBELISING LAUREATES
. . . many things we can do but know we should not . . .

It might be a good thing if some Nobel Laureates were de-Nobel-ised for cause, and this procedure could be started with the 1961 winner, Melvin Calvin, the University of California chemist who was given his prize for his work in photosynthesis, one of the basic plant-growth processes without which there would be no life on our planet.

Calvin's headline-making suggestion at the recent Centennial meeting of the American Chemical Society was to get gasoline directly from certain trees called *avaloz* which would be planted by the many millions as a feasible alternative to oil wells. The trees would be milked, and a steady drip of a petroleum-like substance would be collected, transported to refineries and then processed for sale at the pump. After all, it takes Nature 100-million years or so to produce petroleum from decayed vegetation mainly. Why not hurry the process a bit?

But imagine! Here we are in a world of 4,000-million people, with another 75-million or so being added yearly; and every arable acre capable of growing food becomes more precious daily. It is stupid and absurd even to consider giving over millions of acres to produce petroleum which, in turn, produces the smut that destroys the processes of photosynthesis without which no vegetation at all can grow.

Calvin gets a Nobel Prize for his work in photosynthesis, and fifteen years later, as a chemical eminence, proposes a project which hampers photosynthesis.

He maintains that his petroleum trees can grow on desert land 'unsuitable for farming.' So what of the Israeli desert projects and their reclamations? If petroleum trees can grow on desert land, surely our technological abilities can develop methods for the desert growth of food-producing trees and other crops. This is surely more of a challenge to our technological savants than Calvin's proposals.

Energy-supplies are certainly needed. But at the cost of potentially food-producing acres??? Is this the best the Nobel savant can propose? I am not saying that gasoline trees cannot be grown, perhaps even in economic competition with present petroleum-costs. And, after all, there are pulp-tree and rubber-tree forests— so why not a gasoline-tree forest? But that's not the point.

There are many things we can now do which we know we should not, and must not, do. Have we not yet learned that just because we believe that something *can* be done is, in itself, insufficient reason for it *to* be done? The *ability* to perform does not impose upon us the *necessity* to perform.

All of us know that gasoline is a polluter of air, water, vegeta-tion—and people. Do we need more gasoline or less gasoline to fuel our way-of-life? We need less, not more. We need different sources of energy, not those very same sources which we all know to be increasingly harmful to us. For a Nobel Laureate to propose adding to the problem rather than subtracting from it should be sufficient reason for his public de-Nobelisation.

ON QUALITATIVE AND QUANTITATIVE DIFFERENCES

. . . we have become much too quantitative in our evaluations . . .

It is beyond belief that anyone wants an end to human life on this planet in another ten, or another hundred, or another thousand years.

And yet for too long a time the question of human continuation has been approached by doom-sayers from a quantitative frame-of-reference; and from this reference their projections have much validity. After all, given a finite planet with finite resources, a time is reached when the planet is exhausted.

And yet too, does it seem at all possible that despite our demon-strated capabilities in so many areas we should be defeated—as we most certainly are at present — by population-problems? Perhaps the lens through which we view these specific problems needs to be more microscopic than telescopic. Through the telescope we can see only the bio-mass — thousands of millions of people compressed into one field of our vision — for which we believe there can be only man-made mass-solutions. Through the microscope, in this analogy, we can see individuals and identify ourselves with individuals in more human terms which is not possible for us to do with numbers which are so immense as to overwhelm us. When we identify our selves with individuals our sense of our own capability and hope toward them, and our selves, is qualitatively different than our sense of capability toward the mass, toward the immensity of numbers. The problems are indeed immense; but this does not mean that immense mass solutions, so to speak, can resolve them.

The actuality does confront us that unless population-problems are solved the assumption of life's continuation is steadily weakened. The problems are more than only quantitative; qualitative ingredients also *must* be considered.

It is a fact that we have become much too quantitative in our evaluations of most of the problems stemming from population-pressures: How much arable land or fossil fuel or water do we have available for how many people? These are valid points. However, they are not of themselves sufficient to lend guidance to our efforts because the quantitative is not the only frame-of-reference available to us. For instance, the quantity of individuals our planet can sustain is surely a vital factor in determining the 'quality of life'; but it is not the only factor. A qualitative view of these problems may lead us to different solutions — for indeed solutions simply need to be forthcoming. How we seek them, and the areas in which we seek them determines many aspects of the quality of our own lives.

For instance: It is surely ridiculous to assume that the mere reduction of the numbers of people on our planet would automatically improve the quality of our lives. There is much more to this question of quality than mere numbers: the creative expression within individuals is surely one of the basic determiners of the quality of one's life. The hunger for creative expression lies deep within the human spirit. When this hunger is assuaged through the ingestion of plastic pap which is all about us, the spirit falters and we stumble along from one glittering enticement to another. And stumbling does not enhance the quality of anyone's life. The entire world, including the most materially backward of countries, could become technologicalised, and the spirit continue to falter. The question of the goodlife, which is essentially a qualitative question, cannot be answered through technology alone, however useful it can be materially. But one does not live by bread alone; and of course without bread one does not live at all. But life should be more than only survival, more than only existence.

It is within this complex spectrum of human capability that qualitative frames-of-reference to the question of our continuation on Earth do modify our acceptance of those solutions which are only quantitative. The modification is through our recognition that the essential ingredient of humaneness simply must be part of any solutions. This recognition rises within all our thoughts and hopes, however inarticulately expressed, to which we simply must give heed in our acceptance of any attempted solutions.

When we restrict ourselves to near-total dependence upon quantitative solutions our human projectability grows askew within us, especially within those areas concerned with the uniqueness of human existence on this life-giving planet.

It is surely obvious that thought concerning the goodlife, concerning Being and Existence, so vital to us in terms of self-guidance, is far more qualitative than quantitative in its essence; and that if we so desire our intelligence can be far more qualitative than it has proven to be. However dormant such qualitative intelligence may be within us, we possess it as one of the unique ingredients essential to our continuation and, especially, our much needed evolvement.

FUTURISTS AND FALLACIES
. . . a preconceived future . . .

Futuristics has become a popular subject in industry and on campuses. Industry believes that it is a useful tool for projecting future consumer-wants. Colleges and universities find the subject of futuristics to be of increasing interest to students in search of a later profession. Futurists are professionally engaged in using present data to make forecasts in many areas about the next ten, twenty, fifty and more years.

In my view Futuristics can be a rather dangerous tool for many reasons. First off, the more we learn the more we realise that much of our data is less certain and exact than we once thought; and the Kurdestani proverb once again comes to mind—that one can build a wall reaching to the heavens, but if the first brick is askew the entire structure will be askew and will collapse before it can ever reach the heavens.

Secondly, futurists separate the present from the future as though the present, to them, is much too unpalatable; yet they can use only the data available to them in this unpalatable present. There is a curious fallacy here which makes their projections rather escapist in nature and which leads them to other fallacies and banalities. The Limits to Growth is one such example here: Growth is organic to all biological organisms; expansion, however, is not organic to biological organisms. The differences between growth and expansion are very important in any futurist projections.

However, the basic danger which I see in Futuristics is that the individual within such projections becomes a statistical datum which is fed into all sorts of calculations. Projections made from calculations which disregard the individual human being possessing evolvement-capability cannot be at all beneficial to the human continuation.

When futurists discuss the shape of the world ten, twenty, fifty and more years hence, they either disregard, or become professionally unconcerned with, *the constantly changing present* in terms of individual human beings.

When industry uses Futuristics to project consumer-wants, these wants can be stimulated in people through all sorts of devices of persuasion, and industry is adept at using these devices. *And so is government.*

If futurist-projections are taken seriously by people, especially by educators, education itself is then directed toward a preconceived future — a future qualitatively and quantitatively different than the present. And the present is disregarded; education for the ever-changing present is also disregarded. It is as though the future is far more seductive to think about than the realities of the present, and the present planetary violence.

For instance: Futurists are increasingly concerned with the nuclear dangers which will confront the world ten, twenty, fifty and more years hence. This is surely a valid concern. But what of those nuclear dangers which presently exist and which have existed now for decades? What of the *present* proliferation of nuclear dangers and threats presently under way throughout the world? And, especially, what effects do these dangers and threats have upon us *now*, in our own present? and in ways both gross and subtle. Surely this question carries enormous impact in terms of futuristics and the human response ten, twenty, fifty years hence.

The future will not suddenly spring upon us; the future is incremental. We dare not forget, ever, that the future grows out of the ongoing ever-changing present.

ON SOVEREIGNTY AND TECHNOLOGY
. . . *a qualitatively different attitude toward the machine* . . .

'The people' as a descriptive political/economic/sociological term has undergone a qualitative change in meaning. At one time it was descriptive of the will of the people to aspire toward the good; and the phrase 'sovereignty of the people' had a ring of liberty and destiny and wholeness about it. Today this term applies more to consensus, to majority numbers, and to statistical representations.

For 'the people' now to be even theoretically sovereign and capable of determining their own destiny—whether Manifest or Manifestoed—a qualitatively different attitude toward Technology would need to emerge within 'the people,' within us and those who govern us.

The computer (a word used here to describe the proliferating devices for the storage, instant retrieval and manipulation of data) is capable of ingesting millions of units of data fed into it by human beings who need to break down into segmented bits all information usable by the computer. The gross information is gathered by others who too often believe it is their right, because of computer-needs, to penetrate into all possible public and private areas of individuals composing 'the people.' The technicians are directed by others who, at best, want to know answers which will help the governing controllers to determine all sorts of policies for their people.

Under conditions of non-invasion of the individual the computer is a useful, even essential, tool in a complex world of more than 4,000-million people provided that those in power are themselves not governed by the computer but by their deep understanding of 'the people's' aspirations toward the good. Such understanding does not emerge from computer-readouts but from a profound non-mechanistic awareness—a humane moral awareness—of 'the people' as individual human beings.

This is difficult to achieve when there is such increasing dependence upon the machine that the universal language in government and industry is now the computer-readout, with only different national and special-interest accents, so to speak. The difficulty is compounded because the computer, however sophisticated, is limited and measurable as all machines are. When we depend upon it to determine human aspirations we then become limited and measurable.

For 'the sovereignty of the people' to have even theoretical meaning, the non-measurability of the individual must be held in the very highest esteem. And present dependence upon the computer, in the West and the East, makes this quite impossible, even with the best of ideological intentions.

A qualitatively different attitude toward the machine needs to emerge. Such emergence can occur, in my view, only incrementally through Education in its largest meaning (not necessarily synonymous with 'schooling') through which the individual exposes himself with a sense of urgency to thought, concern, and humane responsibility toward himself and his world. It is only through such Education — of our selves, of the young, of our governing leaders — that we may be able to use the computer while simultaneously being capable of transcending its constraints.

Of course this is a large expectation, but not beyond hope, despite the often chasmic difference between hope and expectation. Without such an emergence the chasm becomes ever wider and we become ever smaller and more easily ingestible by the machine. Actually however, such an emergence is beginning to happen here and there, in the East and the West, as people of conscience and growing awareness seek, in their various ways, deeper non-mechanistic meanings for themselves and for an elusive wholeness.

ON MATHEMATICAL MODELS
. . . subservience to the logicality of the machine . . .

The complex logicality of the advanced mathematical model is one of the scintillating achievements of our computer-technology; it carries logic to a curious human pinnacle. Our mechanised world is a most logical world, increasingly more logical than biological.

The bumblebee is mathematically aerodynamically unsound. A logical mathematical model of the bumblebee would clearly demonstrate that it cannot fly. But, unaware of its mathematical illogicality, it does fly. A highly sophisticated mathematical model, designed by a major aircraft manufacturer to be aerodynamically very very sound, proved to be incapable of flying.

The logic of the syllogism — of the major premise, the minor premise, and the conclusion—has been used for many centuries as one of the devices for the projection of human thought and accomplishment. The syllogism is not necessarily true, but it is logical. For instance: All men have red hair; Socrates is a man; Socrates therefore had red hair, is logically correct even if Socrates did not have red hair. The logic is correct, given certain major and minor premises. But logic does not dictate truth.

Logic today dictates that the mother and the child in the lifeboat, the husband and the friend—and the stranger—should perish so that more water remains to the survivors. Logic today dictates that since we cannot feed the peoples of Bangladesh, so poor in exchange-resources, let Bangladesh perish.

Logic today dictates death. And our mechanised world is a most logical world. Jean-Paul Sartre saw this most primitively in his early Existentialist work, as did Albert Camus in his work.

In my view, the syllogism itself is now inadequate; logic itself is incomplete. We have made it so through our increasing dependence and virtual subservience to the logicality of our devices. Unlike the bumblebee, we *are* aware—when confronted by the paper equations—of our mathematical illogicality, and far too often we then modify ourselves in order to conform to the sophisticated model presented to us as one of the heights of human accomplishment.

I am not saying that the rational is wrong and therefore the irrational right, but that we now need to think also in terms of the a-rational, the a-logical; we now need to see our selves as being capable of both the rational and the a-rational, the logical and the a-logical. While this may be a mathematical dilemma, it is surely a uniquely human challenge.

In my view, before we can draw even syllogistic conclusions we must now add to the major and minor premises the *given* premise that life for us is not a series of mathematical equations no matter how complex they may be, unless we are either willing or forced to enter the mold of the equations. In my view, the *given* premise is that life retains and evolves its preciousness and uniqueness only if we accept and seek the essentiality to us of these qualities.

NUCLEAR ENERGY AND SECURITY
. . . that peace of mind and hope for which we all yearn . . .

Nuclear energy utilisation, in my view, inevitably leads to a police-state even in a country wishing to safeguard its democratic processes. This is a very large statement, the validity of which can only be touched upon in this brief comment.

Nuclear materials are dangerous. Security measures are taken to protect these materials from their being lost, stolen, misused or misplaced, both while at a nuclear plant and while being transported, as they need to be, from one place to another. Whether these measures are considered to be loose or stringent, people who have access to such materials need to be constantly screened as to their emotional and professional stability. People who surreptitiously may acquire access cannot of course be screened for stability. (How can such stability even be determined with the total accuracy required?)

How far and wide does such screening need to go to be effective, to be able to establish the unquestionable stability of an individual, even while his personal rights and civil liberties are protected?

After all, there are now thousands of people who have access to such horribly dangerous materials — and with the proliferation of nuclear reactors (for even 'peaceful' purposes, one should add) many thousands more will have such *legal* access. In order for the authorities to determine their *ongoing* stability, should those people have their mails intercepted, their telephones tapped, and be kept under constant surveillance? And why not? They do have access to one of the most dangerous materials yet invented, lethal to us all — and we do need to feel 'secure' in their stability. We dare not take even the slightest risk that such people may become even slightly unstable at any time during their working lives.

Bear in mind that this is concerning people who have *legal* access to such materials and, thereby, people already known to the authorities.

Now let us assume that a functioning quantity of such materials disappears — an assumption quite inevitable considering the past history of nuclear 'security' even in 'security'-conscious USA with its sophisticated 'security'-techniques and devices, much less in other countries with quite weak 'security'-technologies. Since the disappeared material has to be somewhere, let us assume that the authorities suspected it to be in the Greater Seattle or the San Francisco Bay Area. It would be the responsibility of the authorities to find this material as quickly as possible. We would all want that, wouldn't we?

The authorities would take every available measure to try to locate the material: homes, offices, hospitals, would be subject to intensive search, as would be people. Personal rights and civil liberties would be suspended by the authorities in their search — *and we would accept the suspensions.* And the search would spread and become increasingly more invasive until the materials were found. Let us also assume that they are indeed found eventually — and we are relieved.

The authorities, if they are not derelict, surely already must have detailed plans for such contingencies.

The point here is that such contingencies become inevitabilities with each expansion in the uses of nuclear-powered generating plants.

We are all fallible, as are all our devices and institutions. The total 'security' needed in our spreading uses of nuclear materials forfeits our individual rights and liberties, both actually and also as a premeditated policy-prerogative of our constituted authorities.

And this is yet another reason for my deepening opposition to the use of nuclear power for even peaceful purposes. The total 'security' needed to chain the nuclear beast cannot ever bring forth the security of that peace of mind and hope for which we all yearn.

HOSTAGES — THEN AND NOW
. . . the 'realism' of experts . . .

In August 1976 an explosion occurred at the Hanford Nuclear Reservation in which radioactive americium was being separated from spent nuclear fuel. Two workers were sprayed with this radioactive material which, when inhaled, enters the bloodstream and is deposited in the bones where it interferes with blood cell production, causing internal bleeding and increasing the likelihood of radiation-induced cancer to appear in the victim in about twenty years, according to experts. One of the two workers in this explosion was 64 years old; the other 43.

Since the use of nuclear materials has become 'respectable,' such explosions must then be accepted as part of what is known as 'the cost of doing business.'

That is tragic enough; but 'respectability' in this area brings out some truly shocking things. For instance: A leading researcher in the biological effects of radiation at one of the country's main military laboratories said: 'You know, if I were 64, and got a dose of americium, I wouldn't worry about it at all. It's a very realistic way to look at it. If I were 64, I'd figure I'd be dead in 15 or 20 years anyway, and it would take the americium 20 or 30 years to get me, if it did at all.' What solace this leading researcher's statement must have brought to the afflicted workers and their families!

If this researcher is 'realistic,' would it now behoove the nuclear industry to employ a caste of elderly technicians who 'would be dead in 15 or 20 years anyway'? What of the younger technicians in processes of gaining nuclear skills? Are they to realise in their mid-years that as they get older they will be considered to be expendable? and take solace from this researcher's 'realism'?

Such 'realism' demonstrates again and again how, when a particular aspect of progress becomes 'respectable,' the unpalatable within it must somehow be made to seem palatable, even 'respectable,' for the sake of that progress.

But there is more to such 'realistic attitudes' than that. This biological researcher's statement says in effect that the elderly have already lived their lives and that they are now hostages to the future. Quite a reversal indeed. We used to believe that the young were our hostages to the future—and this was meant in a very good sense; in a sense of promise and hope for the young. Now the elderly are, in such 'realistic attitudes,' hostages to the future—and this is meant in a very bad sense; in the sense that the elderly have already lived their lives and don't matter all that much. What a future and hope to extend to the young! and to those of middle years.

If we accept this researcher's 'realistic attitudes,' what of other biological research people who are involved in extending useful lifespans?

Once again, the 'realism' of experts often bears little relationship to the realism of life.

━━━━━━━━━━━━━━━━━━━━━━━━━━━━━

NUCLEAR ENERGY AND CIVIL RIGHTS
. . . no peaceful uses possible . . .

When a civilian populace needs to be on a constant 'security-alert' as it does in time of war, the individual's rights and liberties are unavoidably eroded. Because of the complex factor of 'security' against loss or theft of nuclear materials, any country's use of nuclear devices—of nuclear power-generating plants, materials processing and reprocessing plants, even when intended for only peaceful purposes—inevitably leads to a permanent state of war against loss or theft of nuclear materials. And with nuclear proliferation such losses and thefts are very nearly unstoppable. This factor of 'security,' so essential within the nuclear complex, leads to the incremental loss of individual rights and liberties.

This is another basic reason why there are no peaceful uses possible for nuclear energy. There never were. It was and remains an obscene weapon for destruction. We were seduced by Government, the military, the nuclear industry, into believing that there are such peaceful uses. But the more one delves into these problems — especially the subtle and insidious ones — the clearer becomes the realisation (first published in the book MAN ON EARTH in 1962) that nuclear energy needs to remain, at best, a laboratory tool for many reasons apparent even then that there simply cannot be peaceful uses for it. And these reasons are becoming ever clearer with each passing day. We are, for instance, only now being allowed to know that nuclear materials buried in Scotland thirty years ago are already leaking radioactive wastes; and with increasing frequency we are allowed to learn of reactor-failures and near-failures; of wildlife suffering radioactive poisoning and death because of their ingestion of their natural foods which have been contaminated from weeping storage-places designed to be so very 'secure' in their containment; of so-called 'minor quantities' of nuclear materials missing and unaccounted for despite rigid inventory and 'security' controls . . . the grisly stories continue to appear with increasing frequency. How many omens do we need before we come to our own realisations and senses?

This area of nuclear 'security' and civil rights may appear to some to be especially subtle in terms of its invasive dangers. Are we then to ignore the dangers and wait to become concerned only after the dangers become virulent? *When will we ever learn???*

The protection of the rights of the individual is a paramount purpose of democratic processes, and whatever interferes with this purpose is quite simply anti-democratic. There is no escape from this basic principle. The peaceful uses of nuclear energy, and the invasive 'security' measures involved, are a subversion of this basic democratic principle — and a subversion which is bound to increase as nuclear devices increase.

What then of the military with their miserable nuclear attitudes and obscene nuclear bomb stockpiles? Two factors obtain here: One is the fact that in a democracy the military is *legally* under the control of higher civilian authority and, theoretically, can be contained. Second, within the context of this brief comment on nuclear 'security' and civil rights, is the fact that the military is professionally engaged in a *policy* of 'security,' and people within the military have already relinquished some of their civil rights and liberties; and, especially, military use and 'security' can be isolated and theoretically controlled by civilian authority. Over and over again we need to realise that all nuclear energy is a destructive weapon in need of constant containment.

While such containment does not at all solve our nuclear dilemmas, it can afford us a measure of needed time in which we can attempt to release ourselves totally from the terror of this threat, and not allow it further to penetrate into our democratic rights and liberties.

ON GERM-WARFARE TESTING
. . . ever more lethal technologies against ourselves . . .

In December 1976, as America's Bicentennial celebrations were coming to a close, it was made public that the military in the USA had been for many years secretly using large cities in the country as testing grounds to study the aerosol effects of bacteria, benign bacteria, released in populated areas: in New York, San Francisco, and other places. When this became public it shocked many people that the military would test its biologicals upon an unsuspecting populace, and its own populace. Some people were very much aroused, as we all have a right to be.

Yet why should this come as a surprise to us? With so much secrecy and obfuscation in government, anything is possible, as recent disclosures testify. Why should this come as a surprise to us when it is so tragically evident, again and again, that much of our technological capability is not for the benefit of Man but for his destruction—for the obscene equation that equal fear equally shared is 'progress.'

Do we not yet realise that once the possibility of biological warfare is accepted as policy in this filthy equation, those responsible for it will find it both logical and inevitable that these germ-weapons need to be tested, and in populated areas. It is to the testers quite logical to conduct their field-experiments in New York subways in order to learn how far the aerosols will carry effectively; and in coastal cities in order to determine the effectiveness of dropping benign bacteria—and thereby also lethal bacteria—into the off-shore waters adjacent to metropolitan areas.

Why should we be surprised when for too long we have not even asked ourselves: What is being done to us and to our Earth?

The issue in germ-warfare is not that these tests were conducted in densely populated areas. It cannot be that. That is begging the issue, because if tests are indeed to be conducted, such areas are most suitable precisely because lethal biological weapons are designed to be used against similar areas within the enemy's country.

Is the issue then germ-warfare? It cannot be that because if 'they' have been or are working on germ-warfare, shouldn't 'we' also? And if the techniques for such warfare exist or could be brought into existence, shouldn't the military and their technologists—charged as they are with the 'security' of the nation—at the very least experiment with such devices, especially since an enemy's ability in germ-warfare imposes upon us the necessity to perform *reactively*? What a strange twist to the imperative of 'interrelationships' in our intertwined world!

All this is surely another indication of what can only be called our individual and collective failure, begun years ago, to lend guidance to technology for the benefit of Man, not for his destruction. In human terms much of our technological activity is indeed a misguidance, a mistake. Indeed, it would make much sense to take some things out of our world than to put more into it, technologically speaking. How can we ever absorb into ourselves the good of what we have, and can have, when the techno-structures keep on adding and adding in a manner virtually random? Are the added things—and the added threats—simply to pass through our systems undigested? How much energy-of-ingestion can we expend when that which we ingest cannot be digested? And who *can* digest the capability for bacteriological warfare and its attendant peace-time testing upon an unsuspecting citizenry?

While people and governments, both 'ours' and 'theirs,' may say that there are certain things they would never do—unless of course certain conditions existed, the fact remains that conditions *do* exist which continue to spawn development of ever more lethal technologies of man against himself.

This, and not the question of testing, is surely the issue within the germ-warfare example. And this too is precisely one of the utterly basic issues within all of technology: namely, that without our moral/ethical evolvement, human guidance of technology — for peace and for war — will lead us further to conditions threatening to the human emergence and ascent. If those within technology, and those seeking its benefits, cannot become engaged with this basic issue, technological defeat, in human terms, will most unhappily increase and deepen within our interrelated world.

And precisely in human terms, it need not be so for 'us' or for 'them.'

COMPLEXITY — THEN, NOW, LATER
. . . a basic world-genetic change . . .

We think of ourselves as living in an enormously complex societal-technological world; and it is so for us. Fifty years ago (with the expansion of commercial radio, aircraft, and so on) many people then thought *they* were living in an enormously complex societal-technological world. And it was so for them. Today, from our present perspective, we look back at 'then' and see how relatively simple it was then; the complexities of fifty years ago seem to us in retrospect to be not so complex at all. Will the generation fifty years hence find our present technological complexity also simple to them?

That is very doubtful indeed because our present complexities have become genetic within us, so to speak. The Bomb and all that that implies has brought forth *basic* complexities which even the receipt of intelligent messages from sentient life on distant planets will not resolve. These basic complexities are utterly different in quality and degree than any earlier complexities in humanity's evolvement. Nuclear energy, plutonium, population-pressures, pollutions, arable-acre encasements, increasing world hunger, space explorations and expenditures, a stupidly armed world with its destructive consumptions . . . all interrelated, are only a few of the basic factors of complexity; and all of them have been occurring in our lifetime, actually within the past three decades—and all of them are man-made. We, people, have made them.

Another factor here is that we have so compressed time that we have less time now for adaptation than we ever had before. This factor has a deep significance of its own.

The central baseline here is this: We, those of us alive today, young and old, confront a responsibility which did not exist at any earlier time. And for the resolution of this confrontation we seem to have either our latitude or our longitude if you will, but not both, and we therefore do not locate ourselves to our selves. We need to know both our latitude and longitude for such identification of what and where we are. Our compasses are awry because of man-made radioactive interferences, so to speak. And we need to check our compasses again and again and compensate for the interferences if our compasses are to be dependable for our various voyages. Otherwise we are randomly afloat in dangerous seas. This analogy, in my view, does obtain in many ways.

And such compass-compensation will, from now on, be a fact in the human continuum; I believe that this basic complexity will not ever leave us—not in fifty years or fifty centuries and if mankind is to retain the capacity for individuality—so long as mankind does not become enmassed.

A basic qualitative world-genetic change, as it were, has taken place during the past three decades. We have caused this change; and it is our responsibility, the responsibility of each of us, to do what we can in terms of our own perceptions and commitments to have this change be evolutionary, not mutational. All evolutionary change requires a span of time for its emergence; and time for us, especially technological time, has become quite compressed, almost logarithmically. For instance: No sooner does one technological change occur which affects our lives than it is rapidly followed by another. We scarcely have time to absorb the first one before the second is upon us.

And yet it is our individual responsibility, and life-enhancing challenge too, to attempt to expand our own evolutionary time despite the compressions. How to do this is not simple, and we each must find our own way, make our own compass-compensations, even as we know that we are part of the entire history of all life and, that whatever we do, we add our contribution to it for good or ill.

THE ARREST OF FAILURE
. . . deliberately to seek the good . . .

Are we in process of arresting our human failures and the failure of the Man/Earth interrelationship? Is the continuing and quite apparent failure of that interrelationship of such momentum that the effects of our arresting-processes are too insignificant to be discerned?

Throughout the world people in increasing numbers are aware of the failure; they are also aware of specific actions which should be taken to help arrest the failure; many are actually engaged in attempts at reclamation.

The technology for reclamation exists; the know-how exists; even a large awareness of know-*why* exists. Yet the failure of the Man/Earth interrelationship continues, with each failure bringing us closer to terminal failure, which could take many forms—from nuclear destruction to the insidious hopelessness of enmassment.

The failure of the Man/Earth interrelationship is a reflection of—and reflected by—the failures in our own lives and our own relationships.

Today, and in the recent past, an awakening awareness of the Man/Earth failure has come about through exhortations. But we are past the point where further exhortations will awaken further awareness, much less deepen it. And we are past the point of waiting for disseminated pain to stimulate needed changes.

Pain, so subjectively definite and so elusive in description, is perhaps the single largest human response presently controllable. The surgical nurse who says: 'My patients are not in pain!' speaks with authority. She knows the various drugs for pain-control. Mental pain, especially in the technological West, can frequently be eased by psychiatric/psychological manipulations. That pain which might visit a person should he or she become aware that this is not the best of all possible worlds, has usually been deadened and excised through early conditioning that this *is* the best of all worlds.

So pain as a stimulant to effect those massive changes necessary to arrest the Man/Earth failure would not work because devices for the diminution of pain are plentiful, palatable, and available. The Soma of our world is more of a tube than a pill.

Fear would not be effective either. Fear that is strong enough to be painful emotion usually generates impotence which, in turn, generates more fear and deeper impotence; seldom does it generate awareness.

We are also past the point where awareness, so desperately needed in the individual and in the entire human continuum, can be generated through technological means alone. Our sophisticated devices prod us more toward the cosmetical than the cosmological.

We are also past the point where we can depend upon external miracle for the redress of the imbalances of our own making.

If we are to attempt to arrest failure we must deliberately seek the good if only because we already know how very bad the bad can be. And what we seek must be the greater good for the Man/Man and Man/Earth interrelationship, within which individual good is not submerged but enhanced. There is no other way.

PLANETARY VIOLENCE
. . . an adversary relationship . . .

We are in the midst of growing planetary violence and, simultaneously, emerging planetary anti-violence.

I am not referring to the strip-mining of the land or to the pollution of the sea or to the contamination of the air. These, and so many other violences, are effects, not causes; and the relationship between cause-and-effect is becoming clearer to the individuals of emerging anti-violence.

Planetary violence can be defined as an attitude of mind mainly on the part of the controllers of many kinds of power, in the East and the West. Their attitudes are formed, in many ways, from data supplied to them by various technological experts whose information the controllers accept when it strengthens the opinions the controllers have of their own political and economic policies and sagacities. However, the accumulators of data are not necessarily the most valid interpreters of the data. I am not saying that technological expertise is to be rejected. Not that at all. Here again, the *attitude* with which such data is evaluated is critically important. And attitude is a frame-of-mind which has large bearing on the frames-of-reference one employs in order to achieve one's purpose.

Because the controllers of power function with the belief that they are in an adversary relationship toward each other, the result is a pervasive attitude of enmity which governs their actions toward the world and so wastefully consumes its resources. And a collectivist adversary attitude on the part of the people of power has emerged toward Earth itself and its peoples — and all in the name of 'security' or 'freedom' or 'national policy' or 'good business.'

I leave it to your own imagination to consider the changes which would emerge upon the planet if power-controllers were not in a steady-state adversary attitude toward one another — and collectively toward Earth and its peoples.

The individuals of emerging anti-violence are from all societal strata; and they are beginning to realise that the *attitudes* of the power-controllers are the causes of the planetary violence impinging upon all peoples. This is evident in the rising distrust of government officials, of industry leaders, and even of the leaders of research and educational systems. This distrust is increasing.

It is not that the individuals of emerging anti-violence seek anarchy as a solution. Quite the contrary. Many young people from various strata are attempting to function within adversary societal structures in Education, Law, Government, and even within research complexes.

In my view they are, articulately and not, gradually becoming unaccepting of the planetary violence they see and learn about, and they feel that there must be another way, another *attitude*, for them to hope to live without fear of the enmity and violence encroaching upon them and upon their own inheritors of the planet. And they are seeking, through many and diverse approaches—some of them valid, in my view, some not—a nonviolent method of adding their individual contributions to a world in discord.

ON GLOBAL DEFAULT
. . . a world desperately in need of unity . . .

On this Earth from which it is not possible to leave, even in death, one cannot exorcise human problems; one must embrace them and, through such embrace, absorb them in hope of developing realistic humane solutions. Of the several examples which could be used here one example, while it clearly demonstrates our global default, also demonstrates our need to embrace and absorb it.

A quotation here:

'Man is a relatively new phenomenon on Earth. He has not yet learned to live with his environment, and actually may never do so, but become extinct long before the natural expiration of this planet, to be replaced by an organism that will learn to live with its environment . . . Let us assume wisdom and honour among world scientists, and respect their search toward solutions of world population-pressures. One seeks a birth-control pill; another seeks new water sources from the seas and even the stones; a third seeks increased farm-yields for areas of need; a fourth seeks new sources of raw materials in remote areas or from new techniques, and so on . . . From what frame-of-reference are they functioning? What are they attempting to solve in terms of population-pressures, even in terms of their own grandchildren's grandchildren? . . .'

The above is a quotation from an essay I wrote in 1960 titled THE GROWING CHILD ON AN AGING EARTH: it is the opening chapter in my book MAN ON EARTH, a plea for an understanding of an evolving Man/Earth interrelationship.

If at that time — when there were some 1,000-million fewer people on this limited planet — Education in its deepest meanings were made available to all peoples and their leaders things might well have been different today. A world-wide attempt at such Education — which, once again, is not synonymous with schooling — using the fullest facilities of international agencies, foundations, educational structures from kindergarten through graduate school, the numerous health professions and industries, and so on, could have done much to arouse early curiosity and later understanding of the Man/Earth interrelationship, and all that is implied here. Even the earliest Earth-photos from the Moon taken in the late nineteen-sixties could have been used in this ongoing Educational process. In truth and sanity, Ecology needs to be a required basic subject for thought and discussion in all schools and governments and industries, and amongst all people, despite the current contamination of this word.

But we cannot start in 1960; we cannot start even yesterday. We can start only *now*. If the attempt at such Education is not made, then chaos followed by massive authority massively applied will surely descend upon the peoples of the world. If the attempt *is* made, could such Education accomplish the needed population-reductions within the next fifteen or twenty or thirty years — and without violence?

We continue to think of Education as a graded system of schooling — and much to our detriment. The American Sequoia made the entire Cherokee Nation of many thousands literate *within three years* through his magnificent invention, original to him, of a syllabary—which is similar to an alphabet but which is a set of written characters each one of which is used to spell an entire syllable, an entire unit of utterance. Within three years the Cherokee Nation had its own newspapers and books. Sequoia, without 'schooling,' was a fabulous Educator. He tried to unify through his syllabary all the Indian tribes; and his untimely death was a profound loss to all Americans. But his lesson remains . . .

Hundreds of thousands of Chinese peasants became literate and then teachers to the villagers during the Long March, the Ch'ang Ch'eng, of the mid-nineteen-thirties when, under the leadership of Mao Tse-tung, they moved themselves, their families, hand printing-presses, small manufactures, across thousands of miles and six mountain ranges each more massive than the Rockies in an attempt to unify China. Much of China's strength today stems from that Long March and the Education the marchers consumed in nourishment every single day of that monumental feat.

King Ashoka of Magadha, India, 2200 years ago, used every military post as a classroom and farm, and every soldier was a teacher. Within a few years Ashoka helped unify the land and its tribes—not through conquest but through Education.

We are—as we have been since 1945 especially—in a world desperately in need of unity. If we start now, since we cannot start earlier and dare not start later, within the context of such Education we will begin to use our truly huge capabilities to ameliorate the global default we now confront.

━━━━━━━━━━━━━━

TRIAGE: THE MYTH AND THE ACTUALITY
. . . 'laboratory rationale' . . .

Triage is a military term describing the withholding of medical attention from those of the wounded who cannot readily be repaired to return to active war until those who can readily be returned are first given attention. The fact that those wounded who cannot readily be returned are the more seriously wounded and in need of immediate medical attention is discarded by *triage*-exponents as one of 'the costs of war.'

There are now people of eminence and goodwill in the technological West who continue to propose, perhaps in even earnest self-agony, that the most effective pressure for the reduction of human births in the crowded countries of the world is for the food-affluent countries to adopt an immediate policy of *triage* by withholding food from those food-poor countries which do not demonstrate effective birth-reductions.

Proponents of *triage* are mainly elderly men (not women) secure in their professions or in their retirements.

The myth such people are attempting in their desperation to generate through what could be called 'laboratory rationale' is that *triage* will force the food-poor countries to help themselves by concentrating their major efforts toward birth-reductions; and only then will the food-affluent countries offer their contributions. Regardless of goodwill and self-agony it is punitive reasoning punishing food-poor people for procreating because procreation has now become an abnormality; however, it is not punitive toward the well-fed leaders of food-poor countries.

The realities of the myth of *triage* in this context generate frightening absurdities. For instance: With the proliferation of nuclear power and its concomitant nuclear-bomb capability in even food-poor countries, will such countries sufferingly and placidly accept *triage*? This is very doubtful. Or consider another frightening absurdity: In our world of instant communication and persuasion the execution of a policy of *triage* (even the acceptance of the threat of such a policy) will so change the attitudes of the well-fed minority that when *triage* proves ineffective in limiting populations, other more direct weapons against food-poor people (even in their own countries) will then become incrementally more acceptable to the well-fed peoples and leaders of the affluent countries with their arsenals of massive death. Will food-rich children be conditioned to believe that food-poor children are their enemies — from birth? If we accept *triage* as a direct solution to one problem, why not accept it as a solution to other problems?

And yet, population-pressures and their direct and indirect implications do constitute the most basic problem confronting the continuation of Man on Earth.

And yet too, if *triage* brings us ever closer to terminal destruction, is Earth doomed to exhaustion and asphyxiation through excessive procreation? Are we impotent in confrontation with this most basic issue?

To accept our own impotence in this area is to contribute to our own and to mankind's failure in many other areas of human necessity and endeavour.

There are no instant solutions to many problems, yet we have been conditioned to believe that solutions must be 'instant' to be valid. And there is no instant solution to *this* problem. We cannot even expect unanimous agreement from present world leaders in government, industry, religions, educational systems, on this issue mainly because such leaders are more concerned with tangibilities resulting from their uses of power than with the intangible concepts of the central nature of a multiplicity of interrelationships of all things and beings.

We especially, and they too, need to realise the actuality that regardless of what we may attempt to begin to do *now* toward solutions, Earth's population will double to 8,000-million human beings — not after but within the next few years, the next 25 to 30 years, and beginning at this moment. Accepting this actuality — beginning with those accepting this actuality — the most massive man-made project ever attempted on our limited planet is now needed to evoke within children especially, and parents and leaders, both concepts and actualities of the Man/Earth interrelationship, of the interconnectedness of all Earth and all life.

Is this too much of an abstraction, an intangibility, for us to grasp as organic to our lives? And yet, and yet — concrete tangible actions toward the good, in virtually all areas, can more readily result when there is a prior understanding of abstract, of intangible, ideas *of* the good. The attempt itself at such understanding magnifies our own immediate lives, and the lives of those emerging human beings toward whom we have willing or even unwilling responsibility.

GOODNESS AND COERCION
. . . the belief that threat and coercion are humane . . .

In the chain of our lives are many man-made links. As our knowledge deepens we may gain more insight into the natural links and into what may be called the 'natural' part of ourselves. Of the man-made ones, upon which we are becoming increasingly more dependent, we have only hazy insight; yet these increasingly dominate our attitudes and our lives.

For instance: There are many individuals of knowledge and goodwill who apparently have arrived at the belief and conclusion that however much a changed philosophical attitude toward the complexities of the Man/Earth interrelationship is needed in the leaders, educators, and peoples of the world it is not at all likely to occur, and surely not in their foreseeable future. To many of them the human continuum is nearing its end and they have reached a harsh attitude toward the human capability. These people and their institutions—many of them wielding enormous actual and persuasive power—form large interspersed sections of the chain of life and they are, in my view, very weak links indeed even when forged with good intentions. Their weakness is not in expertise, which is present in huge quantities, but in attitude and perspective, in scale and vision.

Because *triage* as a solution combining goodness and coercion is finding many adherents in areas remote from its original military-medical application, it is again used here as an example. Many people of earnestness and goodwill are urging upon the countries of affluence a policy of *triage*—of withholding food from less affluent countries, from their governments and peoples, which do not exert massive immediate attempts to increase their food supplies and, simultaneously, to reduce their population-increases. The facts they cite, gathered by experts in various areas, are indeed ominous. Yet they are not urging *triage* because they are in favour of reducing populations through starvation, but rather as a coercion, saying in effect: 'You peoples and governments help yourselves or you get no help from us' in the belief that threat and coercion are humane and the height of present reality; the only valid approach we have and the last resort left to us. There is a surreal quality here which they cannot seem to recognise perhaps because they are enveloped in their own cornucopias, their own abundances which they know were made possible through blessed technological expertise. They seem to believe that they can redress man-made imbalance through more such imbalance in the hope that two negatives will result in something positive.

They quite obviously believe — and they want us also to believe — that only technological frames-of-reference and solutions remain to us; that no other attempted solutions beyond the technological should even be considered perhaps because such solutions, even if valid, would be much too slow. They no longer see the utter need for both the technological *and* the non-technological — the philosophical, if you will — functioning in any sort of necessity or harmony.

They are prisoners of their own past dependencies, their techno-dependencies, even as we are in so many ways. And even if the prison gate is unlocked they can no longer bring themselves to leave the security of their prison-thinking, their prison-attitude. Can we? They continue to want assurances given by the 'enormous machine,' so to speak. Even if their attempts fail they find comfort in their belief that the failure was due to some mechanical faulting, not human faulting, and not due to attitudes emerging from depleted philosophical selves. Can the peoples of the hungry majority take comfort from such beliefs? Do such beliefs bring *us* comfort?

In Steichen's THE FAMILY OF MAN is a photograph of Oppenheimer sitting at a desk in a seminar room and surrounded by bright young faces. The caption reads: 'There is nothing more comforting than a panel of experts.'

In some areas, yes. In some areas, no. Within the complex of areas embracing the human capability, sometimes yes, sometimes no. And therein is the abrasive factor which each of us must attempt to resolve for ourselves if we are not to be self-weakened links in the continuum of our lives and in the lives of those yet to be born.

FOOD AS A WEAPON
  . . . nothing good or promising of future can emerge here . . .

Why is the thought of food as a weapon especially unpalatable to us? After all, it is one of the USA's great resources, as oil is a resource for the producing Arab States. The fact that food is a resource of some renewability while oil is not renewable for all practical purposes should make food an even more potent weapon than petroleum.

Why then the unpalatability?

The fact that without food people young and old starve, and this still offends the American sense of generosity, is only part of the reason. And yet, when American policy in the name of 'freedom' defoliated many acres of food-producing Earth upon which the 'enemy' (and the 'ally' too) tried to survive, Americans were generally quite unperturbed. Of course, during war many things are accepted by participants which they would hesitate to accept otherwise. Yet now, while the USA is at peace, so to speak, the use of food as a weapon is being broached in various ways as though we are indeed in a continuous state of siege against a continuous enemy.

It is within this context that using food as a weapon is unpalatable to many people to whom it indicates that peace is not possible. But there is far more to it than that.

The entire canvas of our being is gashed even by the thought of using food as a weapon. Here we are on our life-giving Earth which we are increasingly realising we need to preserve if human life is to possess even the possibility of continuation into the long foreseeable future. For us to accept the thought that ploughshares are swords at the throats of the enemy, that the joyful harvest is a massive renewable arsenal of war, that the life-endowed seed is to germinate into a weapon against life-endowed human beings is quite actually nauseating: shocking, offensive, corruptive. We sense this in many ways, for we are indeed organic with the living Earth, and even the thought of food as a weapon frightens us to the very roots of our being. How could you even attempt to explain to yourself and the young that the staff of life must now become the shaft of death?

This is not a polemic involving controversy. The acceptance by us of a national policy of using food as a weapon permeates *all* of our responses toward our selves, others, and Earth, in ways which can be only coarsening and destructive. Nothing good or promising of future can ever emerge from a public policy of using food as a weapon. Indeed, such use of food contaminates not only our concept of the land so constantly in need of replenishment, but also language, so constantly in need of clarity and purification. 'Reality' and 'practicality' in this context assume coarser meanings; 'morality, ethics, aesthetics' become virtually emptied of meaning; and the present and future Man/Earth interrelationship itself becomes a mockery. Our need is deeply urgent to grasp to our selves the implications inherent in the use of food as a weapon.

We are all rooted in the life-giving Earth. When the richness of the land becomes a factor of policy to make of it a weapons-arsenal, we all become uprooted. But with roots deep and nourished we can withstand the storms and the winds which are part of the living Earth, and remain alive — as a renewable *human* resource — to partake of its joyful harvest.

A FOOD POLICY
> *. . . we impose enormous demands upon the land . . .*

It should be apparent that because of rising populations and diminishing resources an overall policy on food needs to be formulated. Seventy million people are being added yearly to the planet's population; and our most prevalent resource, usable water for instance, is diminishing yearly.

Colonial attitudes, *Lebensraum* attitudes, prevalent in the fairly recent past are now obsolete; and becoming gradually obsolete are attitudes that any country, even the wealthiest USA, can long sustain a policy of having both guns and butter. The world is changing of necessity because of the demands being imposed upon our limited planet.

Attempts to formulate a food policy can clarify these demands and direct our efforts toward their evaluation and then, perhaps, toward their fulfillment to the best of our and Earth's capabilities.

Before a policy can be formulated, existing factors need to be dismantled, so to speak, in order to recognise the existing components. And the components of a food policy are far more complex than the simple, albeit valid, statement that more needs to be produced not only because of increasing populations but also because much of the present population in many parts of the world, including some of the population in the USA, is not being as well fed as it needs to be, now, at present. And food is only one of the demands we place upon the land — there are many other demands we impose upon it.

For instance: We need land for housing, for timbering and mining, for watersheds and wildlife and wildland preservation, for roads and schools and hospitals and parks, for manufactures and shopping centers — for many uses. We impose enormous, and enormously varied, demands upon the land. It is very doubtful indeed that these demands can be met if they continue to expand at current rates. Actually, they are not being met adequately now, and for many complex reasons.

There are those who say that only massive agricultural production — especially in the USA, Canada, the USSR, Australia — is the best method toward meeting the world's food requirements. And there are those who say that only small is beautiful and is the best method for food growth. Mega-agriculture probably is here to stay, and mini-agriculture and gradations between are having a resurgence. It is a basic question of the suitability of the land — whether for bigness or smallness or something between — and the suitability, if you will, of complex cultural practices. It is also a question of what our demands are; perhaps some of them are indeed excessive. Cultural heritages and practices are extraordinarily important in any formulation of a food policy. To attempt, for instance, to indenture a Dutch farmer to a supermarket chain for his food is as pointless as attempting to induce a Chicago grain broker to grow his own backyard rice.

As an initial step in the formulation of a food policy we need to ascertain and to preserve not only the suitability of the land in terms of its food-producing capability; but, even more important, we need to understand the capability, if you will, of the land's people within the context of their own cultures and strivings. We need to secure an inventory, not only of all the land and climate and water, but also an inclusive comprehension of the numerous diverse *human* conditions obtaining upon the land. The attempt can then be made, as a matter of policy and through allocation, to bring cohesion within this diversity of needs.

However strange it may appear, a coherent food policy can indeed emerge through the gifted blending of the many diverse factors within this complex question of a food policy.

THE MAN-MADE FOOD-CHAIN
. . . a basic change in philosophical attitude . . .

Food is nutritive material ingested by an organism, small or large, for its growth and the maintenance of its vital biological functions. The food-chain refers to the upward biological movement of organisms consuming lesser organisms: plankton are eaten by very little fishes which are eaten by larger fishes which are, in turn, eaten by still larger ones, and so on. It is a predatory sort of chain. Although there are whales — largest of organisms — whose sole food is plankton which they seine in huge quantities through mouth-baleen that act as strainers, the general structure of the biological food-chain does obtain both on land and in the sea, as well as in the air with its bird and insect life.

Man is considered by himself to be the highest organism in this biological food-chain — and preys on everything. (Man, parenthetically, at the top of this food-chain is constantly feeding microorganisms which are near the bottom of this chain. Other 'higher' organisms are also such hosts, as indeed are smaller ones.)

However, there is now a growing man-made food-chain with man-made links affecting all of us materially and also our basic attitudes toward our life-giving Earth. And these basic attitudes affect other attitudes by which we live our lives.

For instance: Food technicians from many countries are trying to do the very best they can within their capabilities to resolve food problems. Their conferences are becoming, in their own words, 'pointedly non-political' because these professionals increasingly want to be concerned, in their own words, 'only with getting food to the people.' Of course they should be encouraged and helped by us all because these technicians are strong links in the man-made food-chain. And yet the very best these people can achieve can only ameliorate but neither resolve nor redress the binding man-made chain biting so deeply into the peoples of the hungry majority—and even into many people within countries of affluence.

The food complex has become so interlocked—with government policies, chemical and fertiliser company attitudes, banking policies, grain brokerage manipulations, shipping and warehousing problems, mega-agribusiness interlocking combines, to name a few factors involving 'structures,' so to speak—the food complex has become so interwoven that what is vital for resolution and redress is an utterly basic change in the attitudes of people who individually and through their structures comprise this man-made food-chain, *if* such people are also simultaneously concerned over its strictures.

Can such a basic change in attitude occur, in philosophical attitude, if you will? *This* is the basic question within the complex of world hunger and food supplies and increasing populations. A basic change in philosophical attitude toward the food complex—and not solely a technological expectation—also means a changed philosophical attitude toward the planet and toward the Man/Earth, the Individual/Earth interrelationship. It is here that conferences and foundations seeking stopgap measures do not fulfill their responsibilities because such measures are only fingers in the leaking dikes of the world.

Our individual linkage, so to speak, in the man-made food-chain is our recognition that basic qualitative changes have indeed taken place within the food complex, and that if we even remotely hope for resolution and redress our expectations will wither as parched grain unless basic changes in philosophical attitude also become part of our expectations and efforts.

If such a possibility is 'unrealistic,' what remains?

CAN THERE BE A SOLUTION TO ABORTION?
. . . more people, more awareness . . .

Will there ever be a foreseeable solution satisfactory to *everyone* to the question of abortion? No, I don't think so. Many other human factors will need to evolve before such a resolution becomes even possible, much less probable. Yet the problems of accelerating hunger, population-pressures, resources-depletion, and birth reductions, are extreme and growing more so daily — actually with every passing day. And it is precisely because abortion itself is so terminal that other issues interconnected with abortion need to be considered and evaluated.

Abortion has now become a public matter, a matter of pro-or-con law. Yet abortion has been used since antiquity and in many cultures. Indeed, some Tibetan monasteries have for many centuries had 'abortion-abbesses' in residence. The ancient Peruvians, Egyptians and others have used all sorts of biologicals and devices to induce abortion. However, it was then sort of a private matter, not a matter of law, either way.

One of the reasons abortion has now become such a public issue is because more people are now aware of the problems of population-increases, world food-limitations, destructive consumption of limited Earth-resources, and other compressive human impositions upon a limited planet.

Another reason, of rather large importance in my view, is this: Until quite recent years unwanted pregnancy was considered to be essentially the woman's problem and not the man's. Women were considered to be more or less subservient to men; and women's problems were then considered to be mainly of their own making toward which men assumed little willing responsibility. However, there is now a growing recognition, perhaps admission, that men and women have equivalent rights and responsibilities; and that in the matter of wanted or unwanted pregnancy the responsibility needs to be shared equally between the man and the woman. Abortion is then not the sole responsibility of the woman.

This emerging recognition and admission of the man's responsibility here has enabled the question of abortion to become a more public issue since men far outnumber women in public affairs, and public affairs reflect usually more of men's attitudes than those of women.

Another important reason in my view is this: Some women of public persuasion are maintaining that it is their bodies which are pregnant and they have the right to do whatever they wish with their bodies. This is a unilateral attitude on the part of such women — an attitude which actually denies the idea and the reality of the joint responsibility with the man of the fact of pregnancy and of the question of abortion. To me this is a retrogressive attitude precisely at a time when men and women need to recognise their equivalent individual responsibilities to each other, to all of life and especially to the life they begin to create through their biological union, and to all of Earth. And this joined responsibility also belongs to individuals who are beyond the age or the desire for procreation.

Having become a public issue, abortion inevitably becomes a legislative issue, a matter of authority, pro-or-con. And it is precisely here that still another segment of individual sovereignty and responsibility is absorbed by the State. This is one of the reasons why I believe that unless we all become tragically enmassed there can be no satisfactory solution to the question of abortion acceptable to everyone until other human factors of understanding evolve. Can they evolve? Probably. But we have not yet even begun to make the massive attempt necessary here, even though the attempts are indeed growing.

To eliminate, or even reduce, the question of abortion — which leads to such a polarisation, such a separation of opinions and attitudes between proponents and opponents—we need to go back several steps to the pre-conception stage of pregnancy, rather than after the question itself has begun to gestate. However banal this may seem it is there that the question of abortion begins, and it is from there that solutions may indeed emerge.

ON THE MANIA FOR UNLIMITED ENERGY
. . . is energy-supply the Rosetta Stone? . . .

If we had unlimited energy-supplies, and let us say, from the non-polluting Sun, would we be better people? and more responsive to the needs of life? Would we conserve our other resources, limited as they so evidently are, more intelligently if we had an unlimited energy-supply? or would such supply actually hasten our destructive consumption of other resources through the manufacture of nonsensical, even though saleable, products? Would we preserve our water and air, and the life-producing acre, with more forethought and insight? After all, however vital an energy-supply is to us, it is not the only resource we need. Would virtually limitless energy-supplies improve our Educational processes? Would such a supply reduce the obscene weapons-stockpile throughout the world? would it bring peace to our perpetually perishing planet? Is energy-supply the Rosetta Stone through which we would be able to understand the hieroglyphics of our complex lives?

Unlimited energy-supply is no assurance whatever that sanity will emerge to embrace the world. Our contemporary way-of-life for us—and also for the peoples of the emerging nations—is predicated upon our having such unlimited availability; yet sanity is in increasingly short supply.

We need to recognise that we are in a world of limitations which, increasingly, and both grossly and subtly, will do no less than change our entire way-of-life — unavoidably. And the question staring at us is: Can we modify our way-of-life *now* in *preparation* for a time in the quite foreseeable future when we will have — to use and, alas, to waste — much less than we do now? Or will we delay and procrastinate until the reductions are such as quite literally to force a change upon us, and upon the ways of our lives?

Truly, what do we want energy for? For the further consumption of other limited resources? If we follow the mania for enough energy, there is simply never enough enoughness for anything. We say, even with passion, that we need more energy, we need more and more — an almost mindless need. What do we need it for?

It is surely the acute responsibility of the translators and consumers of Earth-resources for human use — which means every one of us — to realise that we are in a world of receding material affluence. We are past the point-of-no-return in regard to available resources through which so many of us seek the goodlife.

Yet the goodlife — as concept and sought-for goal — cannot be dependent only upon the availability of material resources. We endanger our selves in the present through such dependence, and we surely endanger our future.

And this, I believe, is one of the basic lessons we simply must learn from the present mania for ever more energy-supplies.

ON 'SELF-SUFFICIENCY' AND 'SELF-RELIANCE'
. . . *our interwoven and interlocking world* . . .

It would be good if all of us — especially those of us in power — realised that the 'self-sufficiency' of nations is not possible in our interwoven and interlocking world. On the other hand, 'self-reliance' is both possible and essential.

An understanding of the differences between the impossibility of self-sufficiency and the necessity for self-reliance would certainly and basically modify our understanding of, and approach to, many things including world conferences devoted to population-problems, to Laws of the Sea, and to food and energy needs and reductions and regulations.

'Self-sufficiency' defines the ability to accomplish one's own aims without external aid or cooperation. Concerning the material aspects of life, this is no longer possible. 'Self-reliance' defines the dependence upon one's own powers and efforts so far as these can be converted to meet need. Although related on many levels, the two terms are not synonymous.

No nation in the world is self-sufficient, not even China in her vastness and present dedication; and no individual can be self-sufficient — not even the wealthiest or the wisest, since in basic terms one cannot eat his wisdom or breathe his wealth.

Yet each nation, each person, can become more self-reliant; and that this must be done is daily becoming more apparent. It must be done from necessity.

In terms of energy, no country can become self-sufficient without abstracting other essential materials from other countries, or without destroying essential materials and resources within itself. The oil-rich Arab lands are far from being self-sufficient when it comes to food and medicines. Shale and coal-rich America cannot become self-sufficient in energy without contaminating its own lands and the planet's atmosphere.

The idea of 'self-sufficiency' for nations or individual persons is outmoded; it now has validity only in terms of the planet itself. And the planet cannot become self-sufficient through proliferating nuclear power-generating plants without becoming permanently poisoned.

The idea of self-reliance, however, has increasing validity on all levels of human endeavour; without it, planetary self-sufficiency is in increasing question.

Imagine, if you will, what would happen if every world conference, every public pronouncement, were to be based on the unavoidable and undeniable premise that self-sufficiency is no longer possible: that all of us need each other. Imagine how many cobweb-like intricacies and manipulations would then be swept aside—at the very least, in terms of Earth's material largesse and its availability.

Self-reliance would then have another meaning to nations which now segment the land and the seas and the human needs of their people. Self-reliance would then assume a deeper impact especially in terms of its cultural meanings—indeed, its humane meanings.

———————————————

ON 'DESTINY'
. . . *our refusal to accept* present *responsibility* . . .

The word 'destiny' has become difficult for us to grasp because of its calamitous connotations. Destiny stresses the idea of what is irrevocable: 'The destiny of life is death,' for instance. But 'destiny,' which actually describes the predetermined course of events, is a word which needs to be re-defined in our present world because we have become, as human beings and even more as Man/Machine beings, the major determiner of the course of our events.

In this sense of predetermination, 'destiny' is very difficult for us to accept because, in this acceptance, many aspects of 'irrevocability' are removed from The Fates and given over to our own responsibility. For instance: We know that The Fates are not responsible for nuclear threat and proliferation, for contaminations and pollutions, for the cancerous growth of fear for the future . . . Human beings are responsible, not The Fates.

There are certain logical sequences in our actions which we allow tacitly to assume for us the quality of destiny in both our private and public lives. For instance: When the power-controllers of the world based their policies on the assumption that equal fear equally shared is progress toward what they termed 'peace,' many hazards and mis-shaping of nations and peoples and, especially of the Man/Earth interrelationship, became virtually irrevocable. The basic assumption in this instance is surely askew, if not insane; but because we have lived with it for more than three decades this fear has assumed for us the quality of destiny—which is absurd—and toward which we now feel impotent. Imagine the changed quality of our lives if during the past three decades the major use of our skills and resources were not governed by this man-made 'destiny.'

In our private lives we more often than we realise inarticulately attribute to The Fates the cause of our own feelings, actions, responses toward our selves and others, as though such attribution releases us from our own responsibility in these areas. In doing so we become ever more mechanistic and subservient to 'destiny' in terms of our responses toward our selves and others and, especially, toward the human future. When we relinquish much of our personal selves to The Fates we make it so much easier for us to accept the 'destiny' imposed upon us by our societal controllers.

In earlier times when knowledge—especially knowledge available to the populace—was far less than it is now, 'destiny' was used as release from ignorance. When our capability for projectability of the effects of our actions was limited, destiny in its calamitous connotations was something we learned to suffer, to live with, to accept. When, for instance, floods inundated fertile lands and killed people, these calamities were considered to be part of the destiny of those lands and people—and we became inured to the tragedy. But it was ignorance and avarice, far more than destiny, which caused the tragedy: ignorance of the effects of tree-cover destruction and over-grazing of upland acres which more often than not resulted in downstream massive runoffs and floods.

Closer to us in time we are, despite increased knowledge, witness to similar man-made effects of our refusal to accept *present* responsibility for later tragic results. All about us are evidences that we are paying, and will continue to pay, for earlier actions determined for us by ourselves and others to whom we relinquished our responsibility. These payments in material and non-material costs are ones we make more to expediency than to destiny.

Of course there are many things which are predetermined as a fact of life: old-age by the number of our days on Earth, for instance. But the inner quality of our days is something of which we are, in large measure, the determiners for our selves and for whatever future toward which we accept willing responsibility.

We are all children, and parents too, of 'destiny'—but increasingly we need to recognise that which the actuality of life determines for us and all others, and that which we can, if we wish, determine for ourselves as we traverse the passage of our own lives.

ON 'NEGATIVE' AND 'POSITIVE' PHILOSOPHIES
. . . the problems have become more clarified . . .

It is becoming more evident to more people that we are functioning in the world with what are actually 'negative philosophies,' and it remains exceedingly difficult for a 'positive' one to emerge. It remains so much easier today to be negative—there is so much about which to be negative. And we scurry in the dank recesses of our minds: plotting, scheming, devouring each other, gnawing much of ourselves and our world into waste. Yes, it is easy to be negative as we look about us. We keep peace by increasing weaponry; we now use food as a weapon; we continue to believe in the policy of built-in obsolescence; we continue to believe that we can 'solve' our energy problems through nuclear devices with their built-in poisonous problems especially in terms of nuclear waste disposal; we continue to be motivated by reasons which are basically negative in nature.

Yet there are many things about which to be quite positive. Indeed, the 'negative philosophies' have unwittingly brought to light many issues of which people heretofore were ignorant or unaware. That in itself is a positive emergence out of the chaos. The recent past has, in many ways, been of enormous education for many people. While there have been many polarities—energy vs unlimited growth, population vs food, and so on—there have also been many clarifications. In my view it is not that the problems have become more magnified so much as they have become more clarified.

We are now very much like the prospector. He surely needs to know what he is prospecting for, and to be able to identify it despite its unrefined state and the overburden in which it is hidden.

If we truly came to comprehend the direct relationships between population and food, between food and energy, between the so-called 'practical' and the humane . . . If we truly came to comprehend our predicament and its many implications to us *now,* our vision would be deepened and broadened. We would look down the corridors of human history with sadness over the depredations of the past. Would we then not begin to feel a surging sense of responsibility to preserve and to purify Earth for ourselves and for succeeding generations?

This realisation of itself places a huge spirit-quickening responsibility upon us *now* which provides at least one central sense of purpose which each of us can possess now — and continuously.

There are many other deeply rooted positive aspects within our own individual potentiality and capability which — fertilised by the mulching processes of the waste of the years — can now begin to send forth leaf and blossom, fruit and harvest, and — reseeding.

DILEMMAS AND EXPECTATIONS
. . . we try to escape through disengagement . . .

When we confront large issues and massive dilemmas — which we truly do — we can indeed see their immensity and become immobilised by the immensity. We can quite actually feel a sense of removal and impotence in terms of our own capabilities to be of any significance within such issues and dilemmas. And yet, to see the immensity of dilemma and to know that we are part of it, however small, offers a different dimension to immensity itself. For indeed, we may say and even believe that we feel removed from the world, nevertheless we continue to be part of the world.

Within the world and its diversity—especially human diversity and diversity within each of us as individuals—are many frames-of-reference from which we take our baselines of expectations and response, our hopes and hopelessnesses. We have many baselines from which to choose; and what are the bases for our choices?

Of course many things are so very interrelated, and isolatable only upon occasion; and any baseline is interrelated with others. Yet when we think of interrelationships we think of something usually external to us: our interrelationship with the planet, with institutions, with another human being. However, there are also inner interrelationships, within our selves, which affect our externalised ones. And these have much to do with our own expectations.

For instance: If we expect little honour within self, and rationalise this lowered expectation, how can we demand more honour within others? within governments and institutions? If we expect little commitment to the good from self, how can we demand more from others? If we say in rationalisation and excuse *of* self: 'But I'm only human,' honesty dictates that equivalent rationalisation and excuse also be applied to other people, institutions and governments. If we are not at all concerned enough over large issues and dilemmas to do what possibly we can within our own capabilities, to expect concern from others is a poor expectation indeed. I am not referring to the expectation of *answers* from others—or even from self—but to that clarity which itself can lead us away from the tawdry and toward that which is life-giving.

I believe that many of us look upon the immensity of a dilemma as very nearly a self-excuse to become disengaged from it, consciously or subconsciously, in order to be 'freed' from it. It is a curious 'freedom,' to say the least, equivalent to the dangerous belief that what we don't see or know cannot hurt us.

We cannot free ourselves from dilemma if we expect that if only we could resolve one single basic problem, all others would then be resolved. And many of our baselines stem from this huge singular expectation. When we find ourselves still within dilemma, feelings of our own impotence descend upon us and we then try to escape through disengagement — and we alter our baselines and expectations to suit our disengagement.

Because of the human diversity, even the most beneficent dictator of the world cannot bring forth a sovereign solution because no such thing can possibly exist. However, there are many solutions within our capabilities which, while not sovereign, do add to the incremental processes of enhanced being and existence.

It is through the rejection of any belief and expectation in a sovereign remedy to dilemma, and through the realisation that we are indeed part, however small, of dilemma — and part of resolution as well — that we ourselves create within us foundations of strength upon which to establish our baselines of reference through which we can, if we so wish, evaluate with a sense of our own potency the many massive dilemmas which are indeed before us.

ON STABILITY AND MATURITY
. . .stability needs to be nurtured . . .

We live in a period of change, indeed of frenetic change, unprecedented in history. Not only change in values, mores, language, dress, personal relationships, but also in the very topography and physical features of our habitat, of our familiar surroundings.

Many of us now thought of as being of the older generation grew up in a world far more unchanging. While some of us travelled rather extensively, even we had a relatively firm and unchanging base to which to return. Cities, towns, countrysides remained virtually the same during the years of our youth. Customs were quite traditional, changing only gradually, and thereby allowing the gradual adaptation factor — the evolutionary rather than the mutational factor — to function in our favour. The pace of living was relatively slow and there was time for reflection, indeed for meditation without any need for schedules or mantras or other similar meditation devices.

The sameness and endurability of habitat and surroundings gave the growing child on this aging Earth a sense of stability and security which is virtually absent today.

This is not a comment on nostalgia or a rejection of the many enrichments of life and health gained during the past several decades, but rather a comment on some basic differences between a child growing up today and a child growing up then. It is difficult to realise that children today are growing up in a world which is not only in processes of constant social flux but also that the very geography and physical aspects of their environments are changing from day to day. A child's favourite hillside may in a few days be turned into a roadbed for a new freeway; his familiar and perhaps favourite tree may tomorrow be cut down to make room for a house or apartment complex. His habitat-vision, what he sees about him, is constantly changing. He does not have the comfort of the stability of familiar surroundings — and neither do we. The young now growing up will think the world was always this way, physically unstable, and to those of us older it is indeed disorienting. The mutational factor now obtains increasingly. And yet, within so much change there is so much boredom and depression amongst the young and their elders.

Why?

Well — while the human organism is capable of great adaptation, the individual can also falter under stresses he or she cannot handle. As individuals we are incapable of growth toward maturity under such stresses; and immaturity then continues for much of our lives and is reflected in many of our responses as adults. Indeed, we are becoming a world of immature adults.

With so many externalities invading our attentions there is little time or energy left for us for our inner selves, for our own maturation processes. And yet it is only within our selves that we can find that stability and maturity so lacking in our outer world. This inner world, however, this inner stability, has to be recognised by the individual as being essential to the child and the adult; it can then be cultivated and tended and nurtured. It is through this inner stability that we can begin to know our place to ourselves and amongst our fellow human beings and within all of Nature. We can then begin to identify our bearings and find our guidelines.

It is this tangible and intangible stability which needs to be nurtured within the young, and within us as well, as a strengthening process which can lend firmness to their hopes and ours, and to their lives and ours.

DESIRE AND INSPIRATION
. . . *sleepers will not awake* . . .

You cannot legislate affection, understanding, desire to learn; you can 'legislate' only the mechanics of affection and so on. The response is then only by rote. Each of us has surely upon occasion, within our own experiences, given or been given such rote-response. It is not especially inspiring, is it?

You can 'legislate' the mechanics of 'Education' but not the inner desire *for* Education. That can only be awakened. And why should sleepers awake so long as they are comfortable as they are? It is deep inner desire that is the master-key which can unlock many doors: desire for Education, for understanding, for affection. And so long as desire is easily manipulated, sleepers will not awake—even to Bach's Cantata.

People who have no deep inner desire are, at best, passive in any given area, whether in Education or understanding or affection. Such people often are closed off in resistance, and participate only through mechanistic responses if they are sufficiently persuaded, usually by some form of subtle or gross authority, to respond at all. Yet from where does deep inner desire come? Surely this is another basic question affecting us all. The Madison Avenue industry, which has invaded the mechanics of Education and understanding, and even affection, believes that desire can be manufactured, given sufficient funds by advertisers. Yet desire of itself may often be quite harmful and not at all beneficial; it may be overbearingly selfish, unconcerned with anyone or anything beyond self. However, 'desire' is used here in its most positive meaning to describe the desire for the good for self and beyond-self, simultaneously.

Often desires may clash within a single individual, and even more often between individuals. But at least desire is present as an ingredient which can form a baseline-of-reference, a framework for willing understanding even when the desires are in conflict. When deep inner desire is absent, many other things are also absent, and banality and boredom reign.

All the educational devices in the world, for instance, all the classroom games, all the testings and doings and entertainments have only shallow passing effect if the teacher and the student have no desire for Education as Education, and not as entertainment or as something both teacher and student *have* to do, and must do because of authority. This applies as well to personal relationships.

So, look about you, and what do people desire? That will tell you more about our world than a dozen reports or a gross of confessional psycho-therapy public sessions. Of course people may not get what they desire; that happens often, for there is no assurance that life is a bank savings account from which withdrawals can be made readily upon demand. Nevertheless, when desire is lacking, or is gone from one, so are many other vital factors lacking or gone.

It seems that deep inner desire has much to do with imaginative inspiration—precisely that ingredient needed if willing inner change is to be effected by the individual; if the individual is to awaken himself to his responsibilities and his needs to change. What imaginative inspiration is present today within educational systems, for instance, especially for children? What imaginative inspiration is present within us so that we do possess deepening desire to achieve understanding of our selves and our world, and through such understanding attempt to effect so many needed changes in the way we view ourselves and our responsibilities, our burdens and our gifts?

If people have no deep inner desire to effect change, change surely will be forced upon them through attrition and authority. Their response is then mechanical, also by rote. And what sort of change is that, especially within a tightening world?

THE COMPLEXITIES OF AFFECTION
. . . more public than private . . .

How we express affection to another, or accept it from another, as well as our desires for affection, depend very much upon acculturation factors to which we are all subject in varying degrees. Demonstrativeness is not necessarily proof of affection; it may be only a social gloss of little intrinsic meaning. It is, for instance, stylish within some current cults to tell people, even relative strangers, that you 'love' them; and the word itself becomes virtually meaningless. This meaninglessness spreads to other aspects of our responses, and our offerings.

There are public demonstrations for and against many things; but they evoke within the demonstrators little affection toward that for which they are so demonstrative — whether it be wildland or wildlife, Nature or their fellow human beings. This is not to imply that affection needs to be present for us to attempt to preserve wildland or wildlife, Nature or our fellow human beings. No, not that at all. The point here is that public demonstrativeness, even for the preservation of interrelationships, has little to do with affection. Actually, we are being acculturated to becoming more public than private in all sorts of responses. Yet affection is a most private individual expression from one toward another which, at its best, is a mutually harmonious offering and acceptance.

A light touch from one person may mean more than an embrace from another. One needs to know the signs in order to be able to interpret another's affection. And it is here that things become complex because so many signs we now use are becoming far more public than private. And who can question that our privacy, on many levels, is indeed becoming eroded through invasion. 'How do I love thee? Let me count the ways . . .' Today we do the counting with a calculator.

In some societies and heritages affection has long been displayed publicly and exuberantly and effusively. Yet despite such displays, enmity between individuals mutually lavish in their public affection does exist. Public affection does not necessarily demonstrate regard as much as it does a tribal gloss.

And in many ways this now applies as well to man/woman affection, as a result of many subtle factors of our making. One of them is this:

We have little regard for our own future, little consideration for the day after tomorrow and for those others yet unborn who will live in the days after the day after tomorrow. And with little regard, we also have very little sense of our own affection toward future—thereby, we have little sense of affection toward our own present; and we become selfish in our responses for which we want a return on our emotional investment, so to speak. What do we then have to offer another? Activities, I would say, more so than affection, than closeness.

For instance: 'Intimate relations' is now an accepted euphemism for sexual action, which often involves little affection. Too much tribalism has invaded this area of intimate individual offering and response, for many reasons.

Whether or not we are living what we consider to be the goodlife, we are alive this day and expect, with at least some hope, to be alive the next day, and the day after. When our future seems to us to be bleak, our sense of potency is eroded—and with it our sense of affection, of closeness, toward life. How can one feel affection toward bleakness? Tribal warmth and tribal security, much less tribal gloss, cannot compensate for the complex erosions of our own making. And it is here that the complexities of affection reflect the long disregard of our intimate responsibilities toward self and beyond-self within the growing complexities of the inescapable Man/Earth interrelationship.

ON CHANGE
. . . we can change our selves . . .

The word 'change' has many meanings affecting us: Change in laws, in public administrations, in curricula and educational systems; in business attitudes and merchandising techniques of persuasion, in television programming, in personal and social fads;

change in the status of one's family and close relationships, and so on. Because the word itself spreads over too wide an area it needs to be defined quite specifically within a specific context.

As it is used here the word 'change' refers to an inner lasting conversion, if you will, in an individual's responses to his perceptions of himself and his private and public worlds; it refers to a *qualitative* change in personal attitudes and responses which the individual considers to be essential to his own inner growth and understanding, and to his feelings of potency in a world becoming more cynical and in a world which mitigates against our basically changing our selves because such a conversion threatens status quo.

This aspect of self-change is enormously difficult for us to achieve for many reasons. We are often afraid to make qualitative changes in ourselves for fear of losing whatever we do have which gives us at least some comfort. Often, but perhaps only sporadically, we would indeed like to change ourselves but find it too costly in time and effort and in many other ways.

Yet many of us know that we and others must change our selves for the better if we and our world are to live harmoniously in hope and promise. If we as individuals, those of us who know that we need to change ourselves, cannot begin to do so, all ideas of the goodlife, for Man/Earth harmony, for hope itself, become pointless precisely because such hope is indeed based upon a fundamental change emerging in our individual perceptions and responses. If we cannot change, what then?

The reference here constantly is to change within the individual, and the central point assumed here is that we can change our selves if we so wish. Assuming that this is for *us* possible, we can then as individuals have hope—based upon our own personal knowledge—of this possibility spreading to others close to us and those distant from us. When *we* recognise its essentiality to us, our own possibility for basic change is indeed strengthened which, through example, can help others strengthen this possibility in themselves.

This recognition of essentiality, in my view, does not emerge within us through external jeremiads and imprecations and doom-sayings which may arouse our fears and angers but surely not awareness of our own potency. It can emerge within us through the realisation that change, as it is used here, does not come automatically to us without dedicated effort; it comes as a result of our intimate evaluation of our lives, of our needs for autonomy in a world becoming less autonomous; and through the realisation that however unique we may feel ourselves to be, if we can change others can because we are, in even our deepest selves, part of a world although never all of it.

Intimate evaluations are difficult because they require a philosophical process, a questing, which is often dampened by imprecations and doom-sayings.

We are in a world of more than 4,000-million people. Each of us surely knows some people so static and rigid in their beliefs that they are quite actually beyond reach of any sort of discourse which may even remotely threaten their security. Our planet, beautiful and fecund, contains many arid areas.

And yet those of us who do deeply recognise the need for change and are indeed capable of essential self-change also need to accept the self-responsibility not to wait in our efforts until a majority is available for change. We need to recognise that a majority, however large, is formed through the incremental growth of a minority, however small.

Change toward the good is an ongoing process. It is when we recognise to ourselves that we are indeed within this process, we enrich ourselves, those close to us and our world with our own vitalness, and nurture the seeds of our own potentialities and those essential to the human continuum.

CAPITAL PUNISHMENT
. . . a climate for killing . . .

Capital punishment is one of the issues to which there probably will never be a satisfactory solution — satisfactory to all. Yet there are several underlying factors here which cry forth to be exposed because capital punishment, legalised execution by the State, perhaps more than other issues brings forth some basic contradictions, basic faultings, in our societal fabric.

Some of us want to kill, through legalised execution, those who kill unlawfully even while we subscribe to killing lawfully through war and abortion and now through the right-to-death laws. We also subscribe very heavily to killing for our entertainment — and for the entertainment and instruction of our young — through television, films, fiction miscalled literature, and newspapers. We thereby justify and sanction killing, murder and mayhem as socially approvable on one level, which is usually at a once-remove from us. But on another level, which is more threatening to us personally, we disapprove of killing as a method for an individual to right some wrong, personal wrong (as is often done on television) or to acquire money or goods, or as an expression of personal frustration or outrage. It is this *climate* of a double-standard of killing that makes capital punishment a hypocrisy. And, are we also punishing ourselves when we punish the one we legally put to death? No, we are not. And that is still another hypocrisy.

In our society killing is quite socially accepted and approved as a means to an end, whether that end is to rid one's self of an unwanted pregnancy or to amuse us in our leisure hours through the tube. Children are conditioned to believe it is de rigeur to right wrongs with a gun, especially when they confuse fantasy with reality. We have developed a climate for killing which has made the lawful and unlawful reasons for killing indistinguishable, confusing, and unimportant.

In this context consider the argument of the proponents of capital punishment that it is needed to deter crime. How can it deter killing when killing is so sanctioned, even encouraged, by society? and where society is steeped in it in so many ways both subtle and unsubtle.

Killing today has become endemic. At one time in the fairly recent past in this country it was both rare and socially proscribed except in extreme criminal cases or in time of war. It will not become a rarity again until and unless society — we and our structures — expunges it from our societal fabric and relegates it again to those extreme cases of criminality and 'just war' — if ever that is again possible.

Consider this: The former warden of San Quentin Prison has suggested that it would be a good thing for executions to be televised so that people could see what capital punishment actually is. He said that it was his experience of viewing more than a hundred executions in the gas chamber that made him turn against capital punishment. However, since television has a way of cushioning reality, perhaps it would be necessary for the public to view executions first-hand, and to see them over and over again. The former warden had witnessed some 150 such killings and he did not say how many it took to change his mind about capital punishment. For some people it may take one such viewing; for others, many. And this is the 'reality' to which we have now arrived.

The likelihood of our turning away in repugnance from killing is not very high—not because society is not repelled by killing, but because society has found ways of making killing justifiable, useful, and even enjoyable and profitable as entertainment. Killing is indivisible; and this too is its, and our, contradiction.

We don't realise how far we have come—far from our beginnings and our innocence; and that we cannot go home again. Some of the things we, as a society, have endorsed, are as lethal to our survival and evolvement as is nuclear poison.

Is it probable that all the killing—in anger, in legalised punishment, highly profitable entertainment—is because we *do* feel ourselves at a constant state of siege, at constant war, with ourselves and our world? It would seem so.

HUMANENESS: THEN AND NOW
. . . today the need is far greater . . .

Are we now more humane or less humane than people were in the recent and distant past?

In the past people were inhumane essentially because they were, in our terms, ignorant. Today people are inhumane not so much because of ignorance but essentially because of selfishness.

In the past egalitarianism as an idea and a societal virtue was non-existent very nearly anywhere. Amongst the Greeks at the height of their ancient culture slavery was commonly accepted. Corporal punishment of transgressors was harsh and immediate. In England, only a few hundred years ago, a child caught stealing a partridge could be put to death. Yet the punishers were not all barbarians, in their terms and in their times. Joan of Arc was burned alive at the stake in 1431 for heresy against the Church; she was 19 years old. Her inquisitors were not all evil men. Many of them believed, perhaps even in deep anguish, that only through holy fire would they save her soul which they consider to be more precious than her life. Thomas Jefferson, the enlightened persuader of egalitarianism, was a slave-owner, as was George Washington and others who presented the world of 200 years ago a monumental Declaration of Independence. Medical ignorance during the past resulted in inhumane practices so barbaric as to be almost inconceivable to us today. Yet physicians, then as now, swore the Oath of Hippocrates with its gentle provisions for doctor-patient relationships.

Man's inhumanity to man continues today despite more knowledge being more widely disseminated to more people than ever before in all our history. Are we more humane or less humane than ever before? Unhappily we are both more and less. Our devices for inhumaneness are both more gross and more subtle than were such devices in the past, and they can be applied more broadly to more people than ever before.

The reason why people are now inhumane more because of selfishness than through ignorance is this, in my view: Today when we are inhumane toward our fellow human being we *know* we are, and we are so for reasons of personal gain—whether for money, or power, or domination over another. We know, as the people then did not, that all things are interrelated; that our planet is limited; that human beings, wherever they are, are individuals with whom we have pleasant or unpleasant kinship. Cruelty and brutality exist now as then; but now we know it to be cruelty and brutality, and realise its deliberateness.

The saver of souls through the holy fires of the Inquisition could have had, for himself, a 'higher purpose' however inhumane his actions appear to us today. But now, in our time, a 'higher purpose' for inhumaneness has been replaced by a selfish purpose. Even when governments use their unholy napalm-fires in the name of 'freedom' more and more people know it to be a contamination of freedom and a governmentally selfish instrument for the spread of power and domination, however glibly the public pronouncements may be phrased.

Inhumaneness then was less institutionalised than it is now, and less capable of becoming widespread. I would say that today there is far more individual humaneness than then. Today the need for humaneness — both private and public, individual and institutional — is far greater than it ever was precisely because of our intertwinings and interrelationships, and because our devices for inhumaneness can actually devastate the planet and all it contains.

But a technological world, a world of products, of acquisitions, of ease of travel and the pursuit of personal pleasure, is a world which actually encourages selfishness in people. This is a factor in our lives which needs to be understood if we are ever to become less selfish in our acquisitions, and in our relationships which we often also consider to be acquisitions, readily replaceable if we so desire.

I would say that we are much less inhumane as individuals than were people in the past. But being less inhumane does not necessarily make us more humane. We can be less inhumane *and less concerned,* simultaneously. And *this* simultaneity is encouraged through affluence. Indeed, selfishness and affluence are interrelated. How true it is that the strongest locks are on the doors of the rich.

HUMANENESS AND AFFLUENCE
. . . a truly fierce danger . . .

Past cultures, even those considered to be highly civilised, were with few exceptions (the exceptions being the Maya and Inca civilisations discovered by Western explorers 500 years ago, and the highly civilised reign of King Ashoka of Magahda, India more than 2200 years ago) quite devoid of humaneness in their societal structures, even though individuals within those times and structures may have been much aware of this factor of humaneness.

Socrates, 25-centuries ago, was surely aware of the need for humaneness, even though the Athenian civilisation was quite devoid of this element. Indeed, Herodotus, the Greek historian who lived during that period, proposed quite inhumane policies toward the old, the young, and the women of his time whom he considered to be useless and a drain upon the State in its struggles against its enemies.

During the past 2500 years no correlation has existed between humaneness and the level of a civilisation, except for those few mentioned. Indeed, humaneness is a word which does not exist in every cultural lexicon even today.

We in our present world have been able to afford humaneness — to afford our humane attitudes and actualities toward others — mainly because of our affluence. With the recession of affluence, will our humaneness recede, diminish and perhaps disappear? This is not a speculative question when we see India today deciding, as a matter of expedient policy, to extend its food program to peoples in the cities and not to those in the countryside mainly because those in the cities constitute a greater threat to India's power-structures than do those in the country. Will other governments follow India's path here?

Consider the present need for humaneness, the essentiality both biological and ideational for humaneness in our present world, and our actual capabilities for humaneness. And consider our comprehension of what humaneness does for us now, in the present, in terms of our many inner and outer responses. And then bring to thought our present capabilities for *in*humaneness, and the persuasion-weapons which are controlled by those who can *impose* non-humaneness as a survival virtue.

The counterpoint between what we recognise as humaneness and inhumaneness is indeed a recent phenomenon. But this recognition has become enormously essential in our present world of receding affluence.

Many may well recall how automation was held aloft, several years ago, as the richest of humanising promises for the goodlife because people 'will then be free to be creative in their new leisure . . .' As with other promises of the technological goodlife, has this one been fulfilled?

It is in the very nature of things as they are now upon our planet that humaneness simply must become part of our contemporary societal structures with their enormous powers. When devoid of this factor, a power-structure is now a malignant growth upon all of Earth.

But humaneness does not become organic to any societal structure until it becomes so to individuals. And the danger of the recession of humaneness within us as individuals, in the degree that affluence recedes from us, is a truly fierce danger. To ignore it because of its nightmare quality simply increases the danger.

To try to begin to understand it now, and to realise its ongoing threat both in the now and for all the laters, is urgently important to each of us if this danger is to be diluted and overcome in our world of receding affluence.

THE TUNNEL-VISION OF SPECIFICS
. . . our personalised fallout-shelter . . .

Each of us needs a sense of largeness-beyond-self in order to retain and enrich a deeper awareness *of* self — a sense of Universals which can lend deeper meanings to many of the specifics of our lives. Despite our present capability to seek the Universals which interrelate us in kinship with past, present, future — and with all things and beings, and our own necessities for evolvement — our vision seems to be increasingly tunnelled by specifics which dominate our actions and our views of our selves and our world.

Never before in all history have so many people been exposed to ideas which are indeed vast to them; yet expediency reigns. There are so many specific things impinging upon us in the moment that we have little remaining of ourselves for the larger view, the larger concern, the larger thought. We then imbue the Specific with the largeness of the Universal.

Is this because we quite literally have so much in need of doing right now that all we have remaining in us is the hope that the later will work itself out? Do we deliberately place ourselves within the Tunnel of Specifics in order not to think of later? Are we indeed fearful of later? Are we rushing through our lives because of our fear of pausing and pondering? Are we all Lizas crossing the ice, fleeing from the hounds baying at our heels? Is 'largeness' in terms of view simply too much for us to grasp? Are we afraid of the perspectives before us because we feel impotent?

But we are in an age wherein the larger view cries forth to be heard, to emerge and be recognised, and to help us determine many of the specifics of our lives.

Is the Tunnel of Specifics our personalised fallout-shelter? with its facade of 'safety'? The tunnel itself obscures our view of our own unity with all life offered us again and again through our expanding knowledge — a unity utterly essential if there is to be a continuum.

There is a seduction and entrapment when we allow our lives to be governed totally by specific needs and desires, thoughts and actions even when for the good; when we embrace only self and our own immediacy. We then become extraordinarily limited to ourselves and encased in a concreteness which hardens with the years. This is so of our private selves, and so clearly evident of our public institutions and controllers.

Specifics apply to us in the moment. For instance: We may take pride and contentment in our recycling efforts — but into *what* do we recycle the used newspaper or the emptied beer can? Is the specific act of recycling sufficient unto itself? I rather doubt that;

yet recycling is essential. Is the specific act of sending food to needy peoples sufficient unto itself? I rather doubt that; yet the food and the sending of it is essential. Is the specific threat of instant retaliation sufficient unto itself in terms of peace? I rather doubt that; yet peace is indeed essential.

Much of our lives is governed and framed by specific needs and desires, thoughts and actions—and quite unavoidably. And when we are done with a particular specific we can sigh with contentment or with frustration, and then go on to the next specific in the usually unspoken agendas we use as the daily fare of our lives, which then become more a series of quanta than a continuum. We are foreshortening ourselves through specifics in our private and public concerns and actions in the belief, for instance, that if we could only do this or that in our public and, especially, private lives all things will then be well for us. They will not be well because specifics have a way of becoming ever narrower to us, ever more specific to us. Our vision then becomes increasingly tunnelled, even as we become increasingly narrower to ourselves in order to survive in the tunnel.

When we depend only, or even mainly, upon specifics for the 'good' in our lives, and in our relationships with others and with this, our only Earth, we leave ourselves with little scope and lessened necessity for largeness-beyond-self; for abstractions, for instance. Yet the individual cannot live his life only through specifics and remain autonomous in any manner; he is not only capable of responses and abstractions unique to him, such responses and abstractions are organic ingredients which make possible the human uniqueness itself.

While Specifics exert a powerful immediate impact *upon* us, Universals have a far greater import *to* us.

ON LIFE AND IMMENSITY
. . . a quality of inner vision . . .

The immensity of life and Universe may weigh heavily upon us in our attempts to grasp a sense of our own significance, of our being and belonging, and of the giving of our self to life which is so very much in need of the best of our human gifts.

And yet immensity has neither human scale nor human perspective. Scale and perspective emerge only through our focusing capability—and immensity is focus-less to us.

Perhaps this analogy would be somewhat clarifying: Earth is flat when scale is small. How else could an edifice be constructed upon Earth and retain its verticality, its perpendicularity to its foundation—and its stability as a structure? With elongated views of our planet—whether from being in high flying aircraft or from seeing photographs taken from the Moon—our Earth is indeed not flat but rounded. Yet regardless of how large our vision, and how clear our scale and perspective, we can never actually *see* the total sphericity of our planet. Nevertheless, through our minds we can know that it is so; and it is from this knowledge and awareness that many of our human progressions and understandings have emerged.

And so it is with immensity. When we place our selves in relationship to it in an attempt to embrace it we focus upon our selves, not upon immensity. And to be able to focus upon self in relationship with immensity requires a quality of inner vision quite different than that needed when focusing only upon any externality. I am not referring to the numerous and varying forms and schools of 'analysis' but to something quite different: namely, to one's deeply personal sense of significance within immensity.

People today, especially young people, have so much more knowledge of the Moon and our solar system than Galileo had; more knowledge of our planet than any of the early geographers; more knowledge of human events occurring throughout our world than early historians had of their world. This knowledge of itself has so magnified the need for awareness and self-significance, especially within some young people and perhaps many, that the need is so immense as to be frightening and often immobilising to them.

If this is indeed so, it may be so for them because of a conditioning-to-immediacy, as it were, to which they have been subjected in a world of instant everything. It is as if they expect the seed just planted to germinate instantly for an instant harvest — as if the seed needs only to be a seed requiring neither soil-preparation or nurturing nor later cultivation of the Earth-bearing growth and maturing processes. And there are people who do look for instant significance through all sorts of guruistic projects. They seek self-significance and look for it here and there with impatience or even resignation in hopes that it will easily be found. To many of us, our sense of place has been stripped from us and our world is unfamiliar to us.

A sense of one's own significance within the immensity of life and Universe begins with a seed of awareness contained within self, not external to self. It too needs self-preparation, nurturing, and constant cultivation throughout all of one's bearing life, of one's need to know one's own significance within the immenseness of life.

A COMMENT ON 'THE QUALITY-OF-LIFE'
. . . no longer an abstract question . . .

In a world where we are daily subjected from all sides to inequalities and oppressive indignities, the question of an inner quality-of-life is unavoidably important — difficult to achieve and maintain, but absolutely vital.

The ongoing exhaustion of Earth's resources is reflected in many subtle ways in our personal/emotional exhaustion in terms of self, in terms of our relationships with others and with the world around us, and especially in terms of our sense of failure. This, to me, is more than sufficient reason for us to realise that the positive, mainly non-measurable, aspects of the quality-of-life become increasingly important to each of us as individuals; important within the context of *its* subjective meanings to us, and *our* subjective meanings to ourselves.

A 'bad' quality-of-life—that is, its negative aspects of hunger, poverty, ill-health, homelessness, frustration, and ever-present anxiety—is increasing throughout this country and across the world. Most of us feel helpless to ameliorate this negative trend, and we feel a deepening cynicism toward the controllers of governmental/industrial bureaucracies whenever they speak of 'enhancing the quality-of-life' of those trapped in its negative strictures. Our disbelief, much too often proven to be valid, widens our sense of estrangement.

In my view, it is precisely here that the question of an inner quality-of-life assumes deep importance and significance, and for this basic reason: If we are indeed concerned with what the positive aspects of life mean to us individually (especially those non-measurable aspects) we are simultaneously concerned with what the 'good' means to us, with what 'ideals' mean to us, personally and intimately.

(Are there 'bad ideals'? Of course there are. The Nazis, with their bad ideals, murdered millions. And there are similar examples closer to hand in history.)

Without attempting to define 'good' and 'bad' at this point, it is obvious that bad ideals lead to bad ethics which, in turn, lead to bad actions. We've all seen evidences of this on the political level. It is also true on a personal level. And it is intimately true regarding the non-enhancement of the quality of one's own life and the lives of others. Bad personal ideals cannot enhance the quality of anyone's life; good ideals may.

So it seems to me that the question of the positive aspects of the quality-of-life, especially those that are non-measurable, now contains an intimate vitalness and pressing importance. When we of this country, where most of us are still reasonably well-fed and many not, ask this question of ourselves and of those who exert authority upon us, it is no longer an abstract question of pros and cons. It has become a question of personal ethics and ideals, of capabilities and commitments.

To be ongoingly concerned with this question is to be ongoingly and intimately concerned with life, and with the living of it on this perpetually perishing — but not yet perished — planet.

A WORLD PERISHING — BUT NOT PERISHED
. . . incremental changes toward the good . . .

While our world is indeed perpetually perishing, it is not yet perished because it is also perpetually attempting to renew itself.

Despite the multiple dilemmas spiralling us down the whirlpool, we are still here, afloat in one way or another. However, we cannot draw up accounting balance-sheets of good and bad, and draw valid conclusions from them, despite the fact that one bad-man can now destroy the world while one good-man cannot save it. And yet, if life becomes grim to us we become fatigued, with hope extinguished; and we then become part of the oppressive bad in our defeated and depressed selves. There is much more to the actuality and evaluation of life than a balance-sheet.

For instance: The bad has surely increased in our world, but so has the good. There are 21-year-old people today who have a greater sense of their responsibilities toward their world than in the past. Ten years, twenty years ago, 21-year-olds did not even concern themselves with some of these dilemmas. Partially this is because more knowledge is available today than ten years ago; partially because young people are learning that, in many ways, the burdens of the recent past, for which they were *not* largely responsible, nevertheless do fall upon their shoulders. They are more aware — albeit often despairingly — of the nature and quality of their own continuum than were young people of even a few years ago.

Today there are numerous governmental agencies on local, state and federal levels whose *public* purpose is environmental protection — something unheard of anywhere ten and twenty years ago.

There are many individuals and citizen-groups presently fighting the city-halls of the country and, perhaps not frequently but surely often enough to be noted, are succeeding in their advocacy of legislation for the protection of wildlife and wildland, human rights and dignities.

Would anyone ten, twenty, years ago have believed that government would even consider imposing anti-pollution restraints upon industry, especially the automobile industry?

Despite the fact that the word 'Ecology' has been so over-used (perhaps as a result of the belief that anything worth doing is worth overdoing) ecological concepts have indeed entered the life-stream, and not only in the USA.

This is not to say that we have so much for which to be thankful that we can now be lulled into complacency; nor to say that we should look only at the bright side of a disc-appearing Moon and ignore its dark side and sphericity. What I am saying is that incremental changes toward the good are indeed occurring, however dim some of them may be to us from our present perspectives in the moment. For instance: Human beings are now, more than ever before in history, quite actually considered worthy of regard and humaneness as individuals with certain basic rights to life — including many people who, only in the recent past, were virtually excluded from human 'membership,' so to speak.

We need to take sustenance from the actuality that an awakening is indeed taking place — *not solace but sustenance* — so that the good becomes more than only a pendulum-swing away from the bad; so that the good retains an importance and validity *in itself* in our organic needs for renewability in our perpetually perishing, but not yet perished, world.

OUR NEED FOR MYTHS
. . . a spirit of harmony . . .

When there were fewer people on Earth and the world was more absorbent, our myths about Nature lent a deep acceptance *of* Nature. Now that our depletions and abuses of Nature have altered its bounties to us, we are becoming quite nasty in our intentions toward Nature.

We can accept myths more readily than realities provided that the myths enhance *us*. Within such enhancement we also enhance the myths; we and the myths are then in symbiotic association. For instance, our earlier myths about Nature enlarged Nature to us—the mountain-tops were alive; the animals possessed a spirit; there was a pantheism within the myths. Through such enlargement we too became enlarged because we could—given certain conditions and circumstances which we accepted—participate in the spirit of the animal, the tree, the mountain-top, the desert. This is not all that primitive an example, if you think on it.

In earlier times there was an equivalence between man and his myths; each was alive and functioning in a spirit of harmony. Even disharmony—storms and floods and hunger—emphasised the harmony which needed to be sought if life was to continue for those earlier peoples, our forebears. The primitive peoples who had certain dances through which to appease the Moon-god when he turned his face away in eclipse always succeeded in appeasing the Moon-god; the eclipse always ended and the Moon-god always returned.

The god-myths were all of and within Nature. Our present myths may be thought of as god-myths by some believers in astrology, for instance; but they are curiously external to Nature. Despite our expanding knowledge of cosmography, of the geography of the Universe, astrology, for instance, takes into account only a very small segment of the Universe, even at best. And there are other examples. For instance: The earlier myths about Nature had a far greater universality than our present attitudes toward it, and our present beliefs that we can segment Nature to suit our self-centred purposes.

Through our saturation of the planet we have eliminated so much of its absorbability—and its and our absorbability of myths as well. And yet, 'Man is a telegonic myth-maker, a creator of fables larger than himself . . .' Our devices are larger than our selves, but what are our myths? How small they are! Yet how large they need to be—because, perhaps not so strangely at all, myths *can* be far less delusional than some of the realities of our own nasty making. For instance: The earlier myths contained an organic aspect of propitiation from the people toward their gods; a conciliation seeking favourable regard from their gods, so many of which were gods of Nature. This was not at all delusional because it evoked a responsibility from Man toward Nature. Ritualised and primitive? Indeed, but a responsibility nevertheless because the people *knew* that unless they did propitiate Nature, they would suffer. We, however, do not seek conciliation with Nature, and we are indeed delusional toward Nature.

Yes, we *are* becoming quite nasty in our intentions toward Nature. And yes, too, that is what happens when myths are shattered—even personal myths. It recalls what Queen Elizabeth wrote in anger to her Archbishop from whom she wanted certain Church-restraints lifted: 'Remember, Proud Prelate, who you are. I enfrocked you. You do as I say or, By God!! I'll unfrock you!' To paraphrase it: 'Remember, Proud Nature, who *I* am or, By God! I'll denature you!'

ON ATTEMPTS TO DEFINE 'NATURE'
. . . *continuing attempts at clarity* . . .

'Nature' is both a relatively simple and quite difficult word to define. It is now used with great frequency within the context of, for instance, environmental issues: of planning and open space, of resources utilisations and depletions, of land and ocean pollutions, of wildernesses and whales . . . And the word itself has many meanings.

'Nature' is relatively simple to define when used with a referent: It is the nature of iron to rust; the wild nature of an untamed waterfall; Nature guides all heavenly phenomena; Man's attempts to control Nature; it is in the nature of the beast; but that's human nature; and so on . . . We do gather some understanding of what the word means when it has a referent.

When used without a referent, 'Nature' is quite difficult to define. 'To study Nature' can have different meanings to a school-child, an oceanographer, biologist, astronomer, bird-watcher, to virtually anyone who has some interest in one or more aspects of what is called 'Nature.'

'To live with Nature,' for instance, can mean any number of different things. It can mean trying to live, self-sufficiently, in the wilderness. Would this then imply that one cannot 'live with Nature' when one lives in the city? Is the city dweller then outside of 'Nature,' so to speak? Does the city dweller then need to bring in house-plants and cultivate garden-plots and take regular walks in available parks in order to 'live with Nature'? Does 'living with Nature' mean living within only the resources and limitations provided by 'Nature' and living with the consequences of 'Nature' without attempting to alter them? Does it mean that we need to live with 'Nature' as it is now? and does this exonerate us from responsibility for *what* it is now? and from responsibility to undo our depredations and contaminations? What do 'Nature' and 'living with Nature' mean? Yet each of us has some understanding of their meanings, however imprecise this understanding may be.

To many people today 'Nature' largely means that which re-mains after man has trampled over it; 'Nature' is then a residue, left over after man's encroachment. To many 'Nature' means something virginal; yet when man even attempts to preserve the untouched unspoiled areas he does something to them which robs them of their virginity. He then manages such areas in terms of dominion, of control. Is it 'human nature' for humans to attempt to control 'Nature'?

The word 'nature' is a noun stemming from the Latin *natus,* meaning 'born,' and *natus* is the past participle of the Latin word meaning 'to be born.' It denotes a certain inherent quality of alive-ness and purity. Yet it is a complex word which is often used, even in the same conversation, with many different meanings. (Someone may say: 'I'm by nature a city-person and I'm not interested in Nature . . .')

Precisely because the word does have so many meanings, it is indeed important that it be used with as much precision as possible, even though it is doubtful that it can be used with total precision. That apparently is the nature of 'Nature.'

Nevertheless, continuing attempts at clarity simply need to be made if ever we are to understand even something of what Nature means to us and what we mean to it, both collectively and individually.

ON EXPECTATIONS
. . . we are misguided in our expectations . . .

To have expectations—which we all have, of course—denotes anticipating some sort of benefit.

We as a people have been led to have great material expectations in terms of the goodlife, of a higher material standard of living. Emerging nations now also have such rising expectations, fed in many ways by the example of the tangible affluence of the techno-countries. And we, in these countries, are now being told by some of our leaders and others to lessen our expectations.

If lessened material expectations becomes a national movement —and there have been indications that is happening amongst many young people and some older ones—we can expect not only to do with less quantity but also with less quality; even to the acceptance of degradation of our environment, poorer health, sanitation and housing, still poorer education, and a general downgrading of the *material* quality-of-life because there are not enough resources or funds to meet all of our expectations. And the material and non-material have become so intertwined to us that we believe that a reduction of quality in the former will also exert a reduction in the quality of the latter. This is most unfortunate indeed, especially since it need not be so.

There are many things we could do without or with less, to our individual and societal benefit and to the benefit of the world. We surely could do with fewer costly cosmetic changes, for instance, in vehicles, furnishings, gadgets of all kinds, a reduction which could in actuality enhance the quality of our aesthetic appreciation.

Having expectations, as the term is used here, is a form of presumption that what we are expecting is our due, something that we can look forward to with some confidence to having as our right. Perhaps these sorts of expectations apply more to material things than to the non-material. However, having expectations does not mean that no effort is required on our part to realise our expectations. And, to the point here, to *lessen* our expectations will also require from us effort, discernment, and the inner realisation of what is implied to us in such commitment.

Are lessened expectations desirable? It depends very much upon what are we lessening our expectations for: for what purpose and for what gain to us. In a world of receding affluence and diminishing resources it surely is not only desirable but also necessary for us to lessen our material expectations — unless we accept selfishness as our basic moral principle.

In private and public relationships it is much more difficult to identify and ascertain our expectations — or even to have them realised — if they are of a non-material sort. While it may be possible to realise our material expectations mostly through our own efforts, at least theoretically, in non-material expectations involving another person, the other person's expectations and efforts are also required in addition to one's own. Such expectations of course must have some mutuality within the relationship, whether it is private or public. For instance, our expectations from our political leaders cannot be met by them unless they share with us *our* expectations — and vice-versa.

Expectations and aspirations are related but not synonymous. Many people have one without the other. In terms of our aspirations we are probably at our lowest ebb because we are misguided in our expectations by our ignorance of ourselves and of our world and by our misjudging the limitations and capabilities of our selves and of others from whom we may have expectations which do not become realised. Deliberately rejecting all expectations from our lives may make us disappointment-proof especially in others; it also makes us, to ourselves, inspiration-proof.

Lessening our expectations is obviously not the answer to anything. Instead of lessening them we need to come to a sounder formulation of our expectations which, while this may be a never-ending process, is indeed one of the foundations for the actualities *and* the potentialities of our lives.

'PROGRESS' AND AFFLUENCE

. . . the relationship of 'progress' and human need . . .

Not very long ago yesterday's luxury became today's necessity to increasingly more people — and this was held aloft as a mark of 'progress,' defined as material things previously available to the few becoming available to the many. However, many of those things which became necessities to the many are now becoming luxuries increasingly available only to the wealthier few. Does this indicate a failure of 'progress'?

This is not an idle question in our world of receding affluence. If 'progress' is defined in terms of material affluence, progress, especially in the technological countries, cannot be expected to continue for their peoples even unto the next generation. England, in its present unhappy material state, is a clear example of this; so is the USA in its economic uncertainties which many persuaders maintain is only temporary. But what does 'temporary' mean to job-seekers who, after years of employment, find themselves jobless; or to college graduates, so many of whom fruitlessly seek their first job for which they spent years preparing themselves?

If 'progress' is defined in terms of material affluence, the few may actually increase their affluence, while the many—even in technologically advanced countries—will be in deepening recessions, initially of affluence and then of necessities. This polarisation, which is surely not 'progress,' is foreboding within any country, and especially so within those considered to be technologically advanced. To define 'progress' in terms of material affluence is a distortion—erroneous and threatening.

Yet progress is a state surely to be desired.

Let us assume a simpler definition with which we can all agree: that one of the meanings of 'progress' is the elimination of hunger. Surely we would all feel a sense of human and humane progress if we could and did eliminate hunger. But in order to eliminate hunger we would also need to eliminate weapons because we can no longer have guns *and* butter; weapons are too costly and so is butter, and our planetary resources are indeed limited.

It is unavoidably apparent that even this simple definition of 'progress' affects all our lives and the public policies of virtually all countries in many complex ways.

Hunger and affluence as 'progress' cannot co-exist peacefully in any country, or on a limited planet.

But let us make the further assumption that hunger has indeed been eliminated, and the world is at peace. The question of 'progress' then assumes a different dimension, a more personal one, involving individual human *need,* which is extraordinarily complex, embracing as it does both material and non-material aspects of one's life. Straightaway I would say that for 'progress' to have meaning, human need, however individualised, must not be contaminative of other individuals and of the Man/Earth interrelationship. (For instance: If someone maintains that he simply needs a monster vehicle for himself, his 'need' is contaminative to others, however satisfying it may be to him.)

The relationship of 'progress' and human need, which has been pressing upon us for decades, can no longer be avoided by thoughtful people if for no other reason than the daily actuality of rising populations and expectations confronting the recession of Earth's material affluence.

It should be, but rarely is, the duty of leaders to help generate, *with* their peoples, an environment where human material and non-material need can be expected to be fulfilled.

In the non-material area especially, we must realise that individual aspirations within the context of need are determined in many ways, and through many honourable and dishonourable persuasions which we need to learn to recognise for our selves if progress is to have individual meaning.

It is utterly vital for us to recognise that Progress — this state of being surely to be desired — *does not come to us 'naturally'* — without knowledge, effort, dedication, and recognition of its multiple meanings.

MATURITY AND AFFLUENCE
. . . maturity is quite actually hampered . . .

Is there a relationship between immaturity and affluence? It would seem so even though there may be many exceptions.

We can recognise maturity and immaturity in plants and animals more readily than we can in ourselves and others. We know that a mature plant is one which is fulfilling its botanical function and that a mature animal is one fulfilling its biological function. The plant and animal do not remain immature; they either mature or perish. Because the non-biological, the supra-biological function, so to speak, of the human being is not at all clear to us, a mature individual is far more difficult to recognise or define. The fulfillment of biological functions does not, of itself, have much bearing upon the maturity of an individual. Indeed, an immature adult human being does not necessarily perish but adds his immaturity as a burden to his fellow people, even if he may be kind, gentle and pleasant.

The reason it is a burden, in my view, is because adult immaturity imposes many dependencies of a transient and shallow nature upon others. In an affluent society such dependencies can readily be purchased, so to speak, with the result that maturity is quite actually hampered and even considered to be a hindrance. In such a society governmental and industrial systems, advertising, publishing and entertainment systems apparently consider an immature adult populace to be beneficial to the continued functioning of the overall system. This is evident all about us, and we each can surely supply our own examples.

When material affluence in such a society recedes, the immature adult does not thereby suddenly achieve maturity; and the societal fabric containing its many immaturities becomes stressed, then coarsened, and then torn. Not only can people then not fulfill their human and humane functions, they cannot even identify them. The populace then becomes more concerned with the biological and the material than with the supra-biological and the non-material aspects of being human.

Immaturity in its various aspects is indeed an enormous burden, however unrecognisable it may be to the immature adult.

A small example of this burden is in the very costly school structures throughout the country and in the high school parking-lots containing student vehicles many times more costly than all the books and equipment contained in the school's libraries and laboratories. Is there a direct relationship between such material affluence and the poor quality, the immature quality, of education within such schools? It is a relationship surely to be pondered by us all.

In truth the more materially affluent a society is, the more mature do its people need to be if their finite resources are indeed to be recognised as being finite to be used and re-used wisely and with maturity.

EDUCATION AND ENTERTAINMENT
. . . the ascendency of entertainment over education . . .

We have entrapped ourselves into the belief that entertainment is an essential factor within education, especially of the young. This fallacy has been with us for at least two decades and it has proven very costly in many ways. Not only are we becoming an increasingly illiterate populace but also an anti-literate one and, indeed, a coarser people.

Entertainment is an amusement, a diversion, recreation and pastime. However pleasant and even occasionally instructive it may be, entertainment places little demands upon us because we are essentially passive within it. Education is a lifelong process for the discipline of mind and character through study. It is primarily not an entertainment; it often places large demands upon us because it does not come to us effortlessly. Education, as it is used here, is not only a right given by a system, it is a *privilege* in the largest meaning of the word and, as such, vested in the individual.

A child is brought into the school system as a subject first to be entertained in the hope that the youngster's attention will be captured and then perhaps the student will be ready to begin his or her education. School must first be fun to the youngster. School must not ever become work because then the attention of the young student will be lost. And 'discipline' is used in only its punitive meaning. This same attitude is widely carried through the entire educational system. And the *privilege* of education is rarely thought of by students, parents, teachers, administrators, as though the term itself has no currency.

It is sad but not surprising that so many college freshmen are required to take 'bonehead English' and remedial reading courses as their introduction to what is called 'higher education.' And, unhappily, some instructors are also in need of equivalent courses.

If entertainment is essential to education we become conditioned to strange things. For instance, viewers by the millions sit passively in front of television tubes very nearly regardless of what is being shown because television programming is designed essentially to be entertaining and to a passive audience. Occasionally programs of educational merit are indeed shown, occasionally. Even then, numerous surveys continue to indicate that such programs capture a much smaller audience than do programs designed to be simply entertaining or amusing. Many such programs are quite actually horrifying with the effect that nausea and horror have become entertaining to millions of viewers, young and old. Industrialists who sponsor such programs apparently consider nausea and horror good selling tools for their products. And the viewing audience, the conditioned audience, actually demonstrates through its product-purchases that the sponsors and their experts are correct in their opinions. Television is only one example of the result of the ascendency of entertainment, of passivity, over education.

One point here is that the more passive we become as a people the more shallow and ignorant we become of many matters affecting us deeply and daily. We are, for instance, more entertained by the antics of legislators than we are concerned over the legislative responsibilities with which they have been charged and for which they have been elected by a steadily declining number of people interested enough to vote on election days. What of Democracy and Education in this context?

But there is something here of yet deeper significance to each of us as individuals. Entertainment is very much subject to passing fads with little permanence; it is a diversion, a deflection, a turning aside. From what are we turning aside? From what are we deflecting ourselves? From the evolvement of our minds and characters? What sort of parent would wish this upon any child? What sort of individual would wish this upon himself or herself?

Education does not begin with the youngster's entrance into the school system nor does it end upon the receipt of a college diploma or graduate degree. For the child it begins with parents who themselves recognise the privilege of Education, the importance of mind and character, and who realise that the development of these gifts is a discipline in itself—not discipline in the meaning of punishment but discipline in the sense of commitment. For each of us, of whatever age, of whatever schooling, Education begins with these recognitions and commitments. And when does it end? Not during one's entire lifetime.

There is no intent here to deny the value of entertainment but rather to emphasise the harm to us all if we allow it to dominate over our educational needs and urgencies. There is indeed a difference between entertainment and enrichment.

Education as a way-of-life is a never-ending gift to our selves which we can indeed offer to the young. It is a commitment, a declaration of our own ongoing independence, a recognition that evolvement of our individual minds and characters does indeed matter to us. Life, despite pain, is itself a privilege vested in us—individually.

THE LABEL AND THE SUBSTANCE
. . . life should be more than only existence . . .

Creativity does not come only from brush or chisel. One does not need to be 'an artist' to be creative; and the label 'artist' does not assure the substance of creativity.

And yet colleges of Art occupy a rather low rung on the educational ladder in terms of regard and governmental assistance, as do libraries and museums which are considered to be luxuries. This low regard may be the result of the fact that the colleges themselves are not as aware as they could and should be of their own place and purpose in our ultra-designed educational systems. Unhappily art schools are no further along than other schools in knowing where they are going. Indeed we are in a time of deep educational confusion.

Consider the actuality that our technological world is confronting receding affluence. Populations are increasing and resources are decreasing. This actuality leads to all sorts of dilemmas and uncertainties; and so many of us confront despair as we see the riches of our life-giving Earth being expended on absurdities and insanities. From whence will come the spirit-quickening inspirations so essential to us all, everywhere?

I very much doubt that it can come from those colleges which train students to be physicians, lawyers, engineers, business administrators, however useful and necessary such professions may be. The mountains of professional information a technical student needs to absorb during his school years (and also the growing intense competition for good professional grades) all too often leave him neither room, time, nor inclination to seek anything much beyond his immediate studies. Individual creativity, during the school years, is often leached out of such students—and all inbreeding leads to a weakened state of 'wholeness' of the individual, of his perceptions of a world all about him and of his 'place' in it. Yet such schools are necessary and important, and not to be downgraded at all. But of themselves they are not sufficient for civilising influences and impact.

A college of Art can be qualitatively different when it is not only a training-school but something more important for the growth and evolvement of the continuation of human life. One does not live by bread alone; and of course without bread one does not live at all. But life should be more than only existence.

The hunger for creative expression lies deep within the human spirit. When this hunger is assuaged through the ingestion of plastic pap which is all about us, the spirit falters and we stumble along from one glittering enticement to another. The whole world, including the most materially backward of countries, could become technologicalised—and the spirit continue to falter. The question of the goodlife cannot be answered through technology alone.

The creative individual may limit his creativity to one particular craft, but this craft is only the visible tip of the iceberg, so to speak. Seven-eighths of the iceberg is always submerged, yet it is the submerged part which makes visible the iceberg we do see.

We cannot remove our selves from the world any more than we can remove an object from space—there is always the space of the object; and there is always the space of self, and always the space of another beyond self.

To help another person reach out to his own creative expression is perhaps one of the greatest of human gifts one can bestow upon another. It is also one of the greatest of humanising gifts.

In a world of increasing dehumanisation a college of Art can be a beacon which can light our passage through the increasing technological haze.

ON EXPERTS AND WISDOM
. . . expertise is not synonymous with wisdom . . .

We function under many misconceptions. One of the misconceptions affecting us in many ways in our daily lives is the belief that experts, because of their expertise in one or more areas, are wiser human beings than others who may not be experts. And we are witnessing the strangest dependence upon experts to lend meaning and direction to our lives. Of course experts are needed in this, our technological, world which could not function without all sorts of experts.

But expertise is not synonymous with wisdom and few experts are wise. The simple proof of this statement is that the world, East and West, now contains more experts than it ever contained in the past; yet we are indeed in a most troubled and unwise world.

When the expert assures you that your sound-equipment is in good condition, do you then ask him what sort of music you should listen to? When the expert mechanic returns your repaired vehicle, do you depend upon his expertise for what your use-plans with it should be? And when a nuclear physics expert — certified by the Nobel Committee as to his expertise — calls for the rapid immediate expansion of the USA's nuclear-power program upon penalty of 'endangering the entire American way-of-life,' do we then accept his expertise as wisdom, and guide our lives in accordance with his expertise, however well-documented? Ask yourself: Is it wise to spread around our unstable world so much nuclear materials which can be used in the overt or surreptitious making of nuclear weapons? Is it wise to depend upon proliferating nuclear power for our energy-needs so long as all the experts in the world have not yet solved the lethal problem of what we are to do with the poisonous nuclear waste we have already generated and continue to generate in the USA, England, France, the USSR, China, India, and soon in many other countries on this planet? Ask yourself: Is it wisdom? or is it insanity?

This is not a rhetorical question because it affects every one of us now, as well as all succeeding generations and all life on Earth.

Why have we so readily accepted expertise as wisdom? One of

the reasons surely was that we were in a world of material affluence which experts had indeed made possible. But affluence is now receding from us; and the vaunted American way-of-life is indeed endangered—which may be a very good thing indeed if we are wise and strong enough to accept both the responsibility and the challenge this calls forth within each of us.

Another reason is that when experts and eminences do speak to 'the people' they nearly always talk down to them and seldom up to them or straight to them. And 'the people' (to use this euphemism) are seldom challenged *by* the experts and eminences in terms of ideas. How then, in turn, can 'the people' themselves challenge the experts? Surely not by trying to become experts themselves in numerous areas simultaneously. It is not more and more expertise which we need, however useful expertise may be.

Again and again, it is not a question of know-how, but of know-*why*. Idea, again and again idea, is the basic essentiality here. And the pursuit of idea is both personal and intimate to each of us.

We have fallen into the pit of belief in the wisdom of experts, and we need to extricate *ourselves* if any quality of wisdom is to emerge from so much rubble of our—and their—making.

SCIENCE—PURE AND APPLIED
. . . an inevitable separation . . .

Skill is enormously important within science/technology; and skill can be defined as technical proficiency. One can speak of a skilful writer, a skilful painter, a skilful surgeon, a skilful nuclear engineer, a skilful research person. The writer or painter may have little to say of substance; the surgeon and engineer and research person may be doing unnecessary dangerous surgery or constructions or research—but skilful people do whatever they do with technical proficiency. (Parenthetically, this may be one of our difficulties in areas of creative human endeavour because skill, proficiency, often does seem to mask the lack of substance in writing, painting, medicine, engineering, research—and in areas of personal relationships as well.)

Pure Science is the seeking of unity, of the unity of Man and Universe. It is an individual process of thought of the theoretical projection of unifying Idea as distinct from thought regarding product and application. Thought regarding product and application is, at its highest, science/technology—not Pure Science.

The pure scientist has always needed to possess skill, technical proficiency, in his thinking processes. But he also needed to possess much more than only skill and knowledge. He needed basic insight and an intuitive sense of cohesion—and, especially, he needed to *be* possessed of a passion for the theoretical projection of unifying Idea; while the scientist/technician, at his best, attempts to prove or disprove the theoretical; or attempts to *explain* the rational reasons why something did or did not happen; or attempts to help make a construct of some sort.

Pure Science has never been a group-effort or research-institute-effort; indeed, any group-effort, at its best, may be science/technology, but it simply cannot be Pure Science. If Einstein, for instance, had had all sorts of computers and radio telescopes and space probes and tons of skilled assistants, would his Relativity Theories have been more Universe-embracing? He had none of these things. Indeed, if he had them he may not have been able to evolve his Theories; those things may well have been encumbrances to his theoretical projections of unifying Idea. And his Theories are still standing the tests of time and computers and radio telescopes and space probes, and attempts by skilled scientists/technicians with all their equipment to disprove Einstein's Theories. Indeed, the skilled interpreters of radio-telescope- and space-probe-findings need Einstein's Theories in their interpretations. Without these Theories they would be mute.

There is an inevitable separation between Pure Science and science/technology. This separation, at its best, is equivalent to a parallelism, if you will. Space, distance, must exist between two lines if they are to be in parallel. If space does not exist between two lines they become one line; they are one line. And science/

technology, which should be a parallelism, so to speak, with Pure Science, is becoming increasingly uni-linear in its quest, albeit increasingly proficient. Its substance, however, remains in increasing question.

What can the quest of Pure Science be today, with our skilfully made devices and technicians? Again, it can be only an individual process of thought of the theoretical projection of unifying Idea; an individual process of thought of the theoretical unity of Man and Universe — Man in his grandeurs and complexities, and Universe in its grandeurs and complexities. For unless we pursue this theoretical unity, science/technology can indeed obliterate even the possibility of theoretical unity because it can obliterate *us*.

THE WELLSPRING OF SCIENCE
. . . the path is so overgrown . . .

Articles of interest and importance in, for instance, 'The Environmental Journal,' the Sierra Club's 'Bulletin,' the 'Smithsonian,' 'Audubon,' and other journals and magazines are often informational. Occasionally they are peppered with anger. I wonder for what audience they are intended. I suppose for readers already aware and persuaded. The articles add information and re-enforcement of belief that something general or particular needs to be done. They are valuable, and more of them are needed.

My own work is not in that area; it never has been. It is qualitatively different, and always has been. I don't minimise the value of information; I use much of it in my work. But my work is centrally 'theoretical' and increasingly perhaps 'philosophical,' if you will. It is an attempt to make connections in the present from present and past knowledge, and an attempt at projectability through Idea. Is such work important to others? Perhaps not very to very many. But it is important, in my view, and vital too, even if it may not be considered by many to be informational enough or sufficiently action-oriented.

I feel myself to be very much in the situation described in the Steelman and Vennevar Bush Reports to Presidents Roosevelt and Truman which, some of you may recall, warned of the critical dangers of relinquishing 'Pure Science' in favour of 'applied science.' You may recall the comment made in both Reports to the effect that if this direction is continued 'Pure Science' will be lost to us as a pursuit — a basic loss indeed. Well, that is what has happened — except that many professional and para-professional people say that a great deal of 'pure science' is now being pursued, more now than ever before. And, in my view, they are utterly wrong, dangerously so.

What has happened, in my view, is that sophisticated technology is now called 'pure science' while gifted innovation is called 'sophisticated' or even 'theoretical' technology. I have talked with people at prestigious research institutes and universities who maintain that Science has never been 'more pure' than it is today. When asked what they meant by 'science' and by it being 'more pure,' they all end by describing technology: recombinant genetic work, space probes, computerised mathematical models, solar collectors, findings in particle physics, and so on.

Younger people in the overall area of science/technology don't see the basic difference between science and technology. Many older people also don't see it. The former never had a chance to know the difference; the latter, in order to keep functioning under their protective organisational umbrellas, eliminated the difference.

So, the label 'Pure Science' remains; the substance does not. In many ways that is the root of many of today's and tomorrow's problems and dilemmas and uncertainties and compressions.

'Pure Science,' now more than ever, especially since 1945, needs to be increasingly more closely related to 'Natural Philosophy' — and of necessity. But 'philosophy' itself has been demoted. And there you are: The demotion of a demotion.

The good magazines and articles are essential, as is technology. And when an especially good one comes along we laud it; but it is still laudable 'application.' And the path to the wellspring is so overgrown with so many things as to be nearly no longer discernible.

Is the wellspring there, still? I would think so. Is it still vital — or continuing the analogy, don't we need it anymore because we can have desalinisation plants; or iceberg shipments (which I proposed during the early 1950's as a bit of a joke)? This question is, to me, not at all banal.

Well, in my work I've devoted many years to the wellspring. Should they have been devoted to the iceberg? The technological reply is: 'Yes! without question!' The Science-Philosophy reply is probably quite different.

CAN WE RETURN TO WALDEN POND?
. . . *astrodomed and astroturfed* . . .

No, we cannot. Walden Pond remains in memory, its only habitat, but the memory can be enriching to us in the present. If ever we should be able to return to the Pond it would mean that more than 150-million individuals in the USA would have to disappear; only a massive disaster could return the few survivors to the Pond — and the Pond would also have been affected by the disaster.

Yet we must never forget Walden Pond because it is, precisely in memory, a nostalgic reminder of what we have all lost through encroachment, selfishness, and through our rejection or ignorance of responsibilities and needed commitments. We no longer can, for the sake of life and hope, reject or ignore them; yet so many of us do.

The point here is this: To 'live with Nature' today and tomorrow and the day after means that we need to understand what we are to our selves, what 'Nature' is to us; and what the Man/Earth interrelationship signifies today and what it signified yesterday and the day before and what it may signify later. The Man/Earth interrelationship is not a static thing; it is a living, changing dyna-mic *inter*relationship. The arrogance of suggested plans to control and divert Yukon waters to more southern latitudes ignores with contemptuous disregard the inter-connectedness of all life on our quite limited planet. The Yukon waters and watersheds are needed where they are, or else Arctic and other changes could be horrendous, and not only to the permafrost. Consider one seemingly minor thing here: If Yukon waters were diverted and irrigated southern lands made arable, these lands would also be heavily fertilised to yield greater crops in order to pay for the additional cost of Yukon water and other costs involved in proper soil-preparation. From these now-arable acres the runoffs to the sea could be so altered in content, compared to the original Yukon waters, as to be nearly beyond present comprehension; and offshore marine life could be so altered as to be beyond recall because these runoffs would take place in more southern latitudes and not in those northern latitudes where they presently occur. The oceans, and their numerous currents and streams, are fragile and rather delicately balanced, as is life on land delicately balanced. We have had thousands of lessons relating to this balance. When will we ever learn?

One of the reasons it is so difficult for us to learn is this, in my view: We speak of 'Nature' and we don't know what we mean, not really. We also really don't know what we mean when we say we 'need to live with Nature.' All life is with 'Nature'; even if the planet were astrodomed and astroturfed we would still be living with 'Nature,' a rather synthetic 'Nature,' so to speak. But, of course, the idea of 'living with Nature' does not mean living in that sort of world. What then does it mean?

It means that while we *can* control many natural factors, as indeed we have, our ability to perform must not impose upon us the necessity to perform because there are many things we can do which we should not do; that, precisely because our ability is so huge, we need to know how to use our ability for the enrichment of the whole of Nature and not only for the enrichment of Man. It means that ability must be organically related to responsibility for all life because all life seeks to live and not to die; and that when we slaughter the smallest segment of Nature we slaughter part of our selves: that part which also seeks to live and not to die. It means that if we do not, with conscience and knowledge and hope, live with Nature we live suicidally.

Living with Nature does not mean that we need to anthropo-morphise Nature in order to give it 'value' to us. Quite something else! We need to anthropomorphise our selves because we are, precisely through our huge capabilities to alter Nature, altering our human selves.

THE LABORATORY AND THE FIELD
. . . hydroponic attitudes toward the living land . . .

We need to recognise increasingly that controlled laboratory condi-tions do not exist in Nature, and that there are basic differences, growing ever more significant to us, between controlled laboratory conditions — at which we are very skilful — and actual 'field condi-tions' which, more often than not, do not lend themselves to controlled human management.

The point here is that we need to place laboratory conditions into their proper places and perspectives, and not to draw blanket and often erroneously applied conclusions from them upon which we will then depend. This applies to educational and behavioural experiments which are frequently popular, and to other similar attempts involving human beings as subjects. This also applies to the land itself since virtually all land-experimentations affect people directly, especially when such experimentations involve food-production and attempts to increase yields.

The so-called Green Revolution is directly to the point here, with many implications.

In 1970 Plant Geneticist Norman Borlaug was given a Nobel Prize for his agricultural innovations which came to be called the Green Revolution, and which was hailed as one of the greatest promises for the substantial increases of food and fibre, especially in needy countries of the world. However, the Green Revolution requires optimal conditions for yields to be increased dramatically: Weather needs to be ideal; soil needs to be in proper condition; and the required chemical additives need to be right to hand in proper quantity and quality. It is only when *all* these conditions obtain that the sought-for yields are indeed larger than previously. However, when these optimal conditions do not obtain, second- and third-year yields fall off, usually to *below* those which the land yielded prior to the use of these innovative management techniques, with their heavy applications of chemical additives.

Optimum conditions have existed but rarely in Nature for the growing of food and fibre, and the human 'management' of arable acres was always essential. While this was so for many-many centuries — in China, Holland, England, virtually everywhere — the earth was a living matter constantly changing; it was alive to the toilers behind the plough. It was often harsh; it was often benevolent; but it was always alive.

Today's 'management' means something qualitatively different in that the earth is more-or-less only a carrier. And this sort of hydroponic *attitude* toward the living land removes us ever further from our Earth in terms of our own ongoing 'natural' acculturation processes, in distinction to the laboratory and 'hydroponic' sorts of cultural processes to which we are so often subjected. I am not condemning the Borlaug innovations, which remain essentially laboratory techniques and, as such, valid indeed. In the field, however, they proved to be disruptive in many ways: Not only did the laboratory promise fail and food-yields in the field actually reduce, the farmers of the small acreages in the needy countries, finding themselves with little credit and less cash for the purchase of the chemicals required for the Borlaug innovations, were forced to sell their small holdings to their wealthier neighbours, and to become dependent upon those of wealth for sustenance itself, much less for any largesse and sense of independence.

The laboratory is a valid research tool, and the question becomes: What do we do with this tool? What do we construct with it since we do not, in actuality, have ideal field-conditions, ideal life-conditions?

The object-lessons here are rather clear for all of us in terms of all sorts of laboratory conditions which we then apply with broad brush-strokes to human beings who — both basically and actually — are not, and should not, be considered by experimenters, even those with the best of intentions, as laboratory subjects.

MISTAKE AND FAILURE
. . . mulching processes for later enrichment . . .

We say that we learn from our mistakes—but I wonder. To our own detriment we seem to equate mistake with failure. To mistake is to misunderstand, to misapprehend, while a failure is a deficiency, a want of success.

For instance: We may try to do something which is to us creative, useful, even necessary. Then, when our attempts are mistakes because we misunderstood ourselves and what we were attempting to do, we don't think of them as mistakes but as failures on our part—and we discard them. We may then try something else, something perhaps more easily digestible to us because we can more readily succeed in it. In doing so we reject the challenge to our understanding and capabilities and experience that is useful and organic to our maturing-process. Only rarely do we recognise that our mistakes are indeed mistakes rather than failures; and that our mistakes may well become part of our own mulching-processes for our later enrichment.

There are two central reasons for this lack of recognition. One of them is that mulching-processes take time, and we are conditioned to want instant enrichment, however synthetic—indeed, instant everything. The other reason is that we're a society preoccupied with success; success in business, in meditation-techniques, in sexuality as touted by the latest authorities—in all sorts of areas which are essentially technological methodologies—and we have for so long confused technological 'success' with human 'success' and have submerged the latter to the former.

Technological 'success' is readily defined and recognised. A successful nuclear device, for instance, is one which fulfills its designed expectations and its financial expectations. That such a device may have been in the first place a mistake for us to design and build is completely beside the point to the technological people and to the nuclear authorities. This successful device then leads to hoped-for success with other devices. And the original mistake, the original misunderstanding of the implications of the device, is compounded, then further compounded.

We *can* learn from our mistakes, as indeed we must because we are not mistake-proof. We have *mistakenly,* misunderstandingly, equated our own success as human beings which, at best, is often quite intangible and unmeasurable, with device-success. Within this equation we become success-conscious, result-conscious, as though we were products to ourselves and others also products to us, each to be measured and weighed — and, when found wanting, discardable.

However, so long as we are organically aware within ourselves that we are not devices and subject to device-evaluations, our mistakes can indeed become part of our own vital mulching-processes. These processes are essential if we are to attempt to reclaim and re-vitalise areas within ourselves which we have depleted through the many harvests (and also the many weeds) of our lives. Who amongst us can say in truth and dignity that nothing at all within us stands in the need of organic reclamation and re-vitalisation?

It is when we seek these re-vitalisations through the application of readily available synthetic additives, if you will, that we begin to believe that we do not need our own organic mulching-processes. It is then that mistake becomes something for us to fear rather than something from which we can learn.

PERFECTION AND DESIGN
. . . our grotesque faith in perfectability . . .

However perfect his machines and devices may be designed to be, Man himself is imperfect. Yet we are born into seduction (and some from seduction) of belief, then trust, in the theoretical perfectability of our devices even when we realise that they will be replaced by other devices which will be even more perfect at a later time. For instance: not many years ago superpowered propeller-driven aircraft were considered to be the perfect large-scale flying device; today they are obsolete for that purpose, having been replaced, for now, by jet-propelled aircraft.

All device-perfectability, designed to be so within its own time, becomes obsolete when it is replaceable at a later time. All designed perfectability has a temporariness about it, which we know by now to be temporary. When we place our trust in designed perfectability, our trust is then only temporary, only in something which we expect to be obsolete. The implications here are rather important.

For instance: In our ascent, comparatively both long and short, the human individual has never been perfect within any past time; and, more than likely, will never be perfect within *any* time, however long his future may be. Man, therefore, in all his past, has never been obsolete and replaceable by any conceivably designed perfectability.

The central point here is this: When we seek perfectability we seek that which is non-human. When we extol perfectability and place our trust in it, we extol and trust that which is non-human, and which we know to be non-human, far more than we trust that which *is* human. We then extol and trust that which is replaceable *and which we expect* to be made obsolete by a still later device.

How can we then extol life? how can we then glorify life and the human continuum, when we are seduced and deluded into trust in even a *belief* in perfectability, knowing that device-perfectability at best exists only within its own time, which may not even be for the duration of *our* own time, much less for the foreseeable lifetime of the human continuum itself?

Consider this as an example: Thousands of people, millions of man-hours, are required for the design, construction, operation and maintenance of nuclear power-generating plants the energy of which is to be used, let us say, for *only* peaceful purposes. (Let us disregard for now that this is, in itself, an impossibility.) However theoretically perfect the design, the construct can be perfect only if we expect perfectability from thousands of people for *each* of their many millions of man-hours—which is both an absurdity and impossibility. It is surely apparent that all conceivable accidents occur as a result of *some* human fallibility, a fallibility organic to Man-the-Individual, and inerasable from him. No device humanly designed, however perfect it may be in its own time, is totally accident-proof. And there are some devices which if constructed must be — not should be but must be — totally accident-proof for the entire span of their use. Nuclear devices are examples here. The point is that while such devices may be theoretically designable, they are not all constructible with perfectability, even theoretically, for perfect function. And the attempt to construct them is itself an indication of our technological seduction and our grotesque faith in a perfectability which we know to be non-human — and, indeed, anti-human.

There are so many implications here in terms of our own human reality and fallibility which we simply dare not ignore if life is to have meaning for us now and for our human future.

ON DEFICIT-COMMITMENT
. . . in the name of present ease . . .

We blame Technology for many dilemmas of our own making. In doing so we take the paths of least resistance in attempts to absolve ourselves of responsibility. The following of these paths is incremental and cumulative, and it becomes ever more difficult for us to return to the baselines-of-reference which anchor us to life itself. These baselines in many ways determine our conscience, our own faculties and principles conceived to evaluate and decide the moral quality of our acts. If one of our baselines is, for instance, that life is indeed hallowed, hunger anywhere in the world becomes an ingredient of our own conscience. And if life is not hallowed to us, hunger and starvation of others may affect us in the moment, but we do not consider them to be a matter of our personal conscience and responsibility.

Our baselines, if long disused by us, become encrusted and hidden from us; and rather than attempt to seek them, we discard them and try to formulate different ones to meet new situations because as human beings we do need some baselines-of-reference, some sense of inner guidance. In our discardence, however, our stability as individuals, and as part of a continuum which we hope will extend deep into the foreseeable future, is ever more tenuous. How can we have stability of thought, of hope, of expectation, when we constantly believe we need to find newer and different baselines?

Stability, of course, does not mean rigidity. Every stable structure, whether of a thought or of a bridge, needs to contain a built-in resiliency—a capability to withstand stresses without being permanently deformed or ruptured.

While we constantly make new beginnings in our lives, this is qualitatively different from our constantly adopting new baselines-of-reference to suit the moment. Baselines, as well as one's conscience, are not a matter of fads or styles. When fads become our baselines we become unanchored and drift aimlessly within our present and toward our future.

For decades the machine—technology in many of its manifestations—enabled and encouraged us to follow the paths of least resistance, and we were seduced, and seduced ourselves, with glowing promises of material ease. These promises are now fading increasingly for many of us, and we need to decondition ourselves from the quite undeliverable promises of technology. This will not be easy for us to do despite the actuality that we are all in a world of receding affluence.

We have spent our resources in a most profligate manner; it was—and still remains in much too large a degree—deficit-spending of Earth's largesse. In actuality, so much of technology has been blatant deficit-spending. Yet we are now generating another sort of deficit-commitment, and again in the name of present ease.

For example: To replace receding petroleum supplies we are being increasingly seduced by the advocates of nuclear energy who continue to promise everyone ease-through-the-atom. The deficit-commitment we and succeeding generations confront with regard to nuclear waste containment and protection, for instance, is being left to succeeding technologists to resolve. And this is being done with no assurance whatever that it can be resolved. This too is blatant deficit-commitment with which we, and especially later generations, will continue to be burdened increasingly. There is no escape from the payment of this deficit — and what will be the coin?

We need to sever the chain of deficit-commitment in which we are becoming ever more entwined. We need to do so if we are not to be immobilised in our search for our baselines, and for that stability as human beings which enables us to be capable of resiliency in a world becoming increasingly more brittle.

READING AND LEXICOGRAPHY
. . . we are all lexicographers . . .

A long-gone essayist wrote: 'The world is a beautiful book, but of little value to him who cannot read it.'

So long as we consider our world to be composed of hieroglyphics unreadable by us, we accept a meaninglessness in our lives even if we quietly wait for a new Rosetta Stone to be discovered by someone else through which our world will become decipherable to us.

We are all lexicographers throughout our lives, authors and compilers of words whose meanings we learn and modify through personal usage. As lexicographers we often dispense with certain words and thoughts as being obsolete to us; and we add others which are new to us for inclusion in our personal lexicon, and perhaps even in a separate section so to speak. With the years the additions and deletions, and the gross and subtle changes in meanings, form for us a book which is our personal sum at the moment — or as near as we can ever come to our own summability.

I believe that we have indeed become rusty in our reading abilities, especially of this book, preferring instead digests with pictures and once-over-lightlies. We have shortened our attention-spans to the point where our reading is sporadic and creaky. Also, there are so many escapist things available for us to do to pass the time of our lives that we rarely confront the reality that our world is indeed our only habitat, that we have no other of which we know. When we do confront this actuality it is as though it were all hieroglyphics, perhaps even pretty to us but unreadable by us. And yet it is in the competent reading of this book that we can ever value the beauty of our world and also be able to learn and to absorb something of the essential nature of life and hope contained *within this world.*

However, it is a book which, in my view, needs to be read in the original, so to speak, and not in translation; and if some of the words are too difficult for us to understand we need to look them up for ourselves in that dictionary which we all continue to compile throughout our lives.

If we cannot read, the book becomes for us thinner with our years.

If we can learn to read with discernment and nuance, with reference and recall, the book becomes larger with our years. Reading, in this analogy particularly, requires devotion and the willing allocation to it of one's time. Because there is only so much time and devotion of which any one of us is capable, selectivity then can become a precious gift—and wastefulness a crime: unbeautiful, unaesthetic, regardless of how shiny may be the glitter of the passing moment.

In this lexicon which we each compile for ourselves repetition—stasis of thought—is a deadweight consuming space more effectively usable for the inclusion of nuance and re-discovery. This lexicon may well be the most precious manifestation of one's days on Earth and, when written, a gift one can indeed leave as a marker of one's passage—and, also, perhaps one's most precious sharing capability with another beyond self.

DICTIONARIES AND DISQUISITIONS
. . . *abstractions require disquisition* . . .

Many words in ordinary usage have no simple definitions and cannot be defined with any clarity through the use alone of a dictionary or several dictionaries: words, for instance, such as idea, humane, creativity, love, education, the good, goodness, hope, environment, progress . . . the list is long and, because of our own haziness, growing longer.

Such words require disquisition, which is diligent inquiry and a somewhat structured search in order to learn their meanings. It is through disquisition that the individual can then abstract or extract definitions which have meanings to him. And there are some words which can have meaning only through disquisition. For instance, 'progress' is such a word, and not because it has so many meanings that the individual is confronted by too many choices.

'Progress' is a word which can have meaning only when the meaning itself is extended beyond the present, especially when 'progress' is toward something tangible or intangible, something concrete or elusive. To go beyond the present requires knowledge of one's bearings, coordinates, guidelines, baselines-of-reference, and at least some sense of direction and purpose.

When the word 'progress' is used to define where we are now in terms of where we have been, of how far we have come, equivalent requirements are needed for the identification of our selves within the present. 'Have we made progress?' 'Are we making progress?' are questions containing the commonality of the need for disquisition. And disquisition requires a degree of diligence and perseverance, and then application.

It is precisely here that the meanings of words begin to have reduced importance to many people who have only faded diligence and perseverance. Rather than exert themselves to inquire into the meanings of words they themselves use, or are used by others around them, they accept haziness of definition for themselves which results in their accepting haziness for themselves and others in many areas of discourse and understanding. This is surely one of the reasons for reduced vocabularies in many people, for reduced vocabularies in fiction and nonfiction, in newspapers, entertainment, and in both general and more intimate conversations.

I am not saying at all that a larger vocabulary necessarily makes for larger clarity; that is not the point. I am saying that the hazy usage of words most assuredly leads to unclarity of thought, understanding, expression, human discourse, and knowledge of our complex selves within our complex world.

Dictionaries are indeed important. Nevertheless, the list of words requiring disquisition rather than only dictionary-definition is long and growing longer. The reason for this, in my view, is somewhat complex.

More information is available to more people than ever before in the history of mankind. Most of this information is by far of a concrete nature, of tangibilities. Most of the new words added to the languages of the world are descriptive essentially of technological and mechanistic matters, not only in engineering and mechanics, but also in politics and economics, and other areas as well. For instance, even in human behaviour, words such as 'conditioning' or 'operant conditioning' or 'response-capability' or 'potential' or 'sexuality' or 'awareness' or 'spirituality' or 'consciousness' are used to describe what have become mainly mechanistic attitudes and methodologies. And yet, words such as these are not all that concrete; they contain aspects of abstraction, of an elusiveness the meanings of which do not emerge through relatively simplistic dictionary definitions. Actually, all abstractions require disquisition for their subtle meanings to be grasped by us.

Because disquisition requires diligence and perseverance for our understanding, we continue to reduce many abstractions to mechanistic meanings. Are we truly more comfortable with mechanistic meanings and the resultant increasing haziness? I rather doubt that, despite appearances.

DESCRIPTION AND EVOCATION
. . . intimate meanings of words . . .

Colour is very difficult to describe in words. Yet there is a mathematical/physical method of great accuracy for the description of colour.

Any colour, however subtle, is a result of wavelengths, is actually composed of wavelengths. These wavelengths can be expressed in Angstrom Units, named after the Nineteenth Century Swedish physicist who first developed this unitary method of describing wavelengths. An Angstrom Unit, used in expressing the length of light waves, is a minute unit of length equal to one-hundred-millionth of a centimetre. The colour-spectrum visible to us—that is, from red through orange, yellow, green, blue, indigo, violet— and all of their possible shadings—is expressed from approximately 3,000-Angstrom-Units for violet to approximately 7,000-Angstrom-Units for red.

Using these universal units of measurement it is possible to describe a subtle colour as being, for instance, of 4,734-Angstrom Units. A physicist working with colour—in any part of the world and regardless of spoken-language differences—would know *precisely* just what colour is meant by those numbers, and he could then duplicate exactly that colour in terms of those Units.

Nevertheless, despite precision, the Angstrom Units are only an accurate description of a particular colour—but they are not the colour itself. Colour is virtually indescribable except in itself, through itself, and not in words. Even here, what may appear to one person to be a very subtle shade of blue, for instance, may appear to another person looking at the same colour at the same time to be of quite another shade. This is so because so much depends upon the viewer, his visual acuity, and his own colour-experiences.

A description, however detailed, is at best only a representation of that which is being described. For instance: An entire 24-volume encyclopedia can be devoted to a tree, yet it is not a tree. Nevertheless, if one has encyclopedic knowledge of a tree one looks upon a tree quite differently than does one who has little knowledge of a tree. I am not saying that one looks upon it 'better,' whatever that means, than does another—but differently. And regardless of encyclopedic knowledge, the tree itself cannot be duplicated even by the possessor of the knowledge.

For that which cannot be readily duplicated in a virtually mechanistic manner, as with Angstrom Units, the purpose of a description, however precise and detailed, in my view is for the evocation—for the calling forth as though from inner seclusion—of a *sense* of that which is being described. The person reading or hearing the description needs to call forth from within himself that which the description is attempting to present.

The point here about colour and trees is also about words such as 'consciousness' and 'awareness,' words which have become incantations to many, verbal formulas for ritualised 'enlightenment.' Yet these words do have enormous validity if we recognise them to be not verbal formulas for ready duplication, but as words of evocation for the calling forth from within one's self as though from seclusion the intimate meanings of these words. For them to mean the same thing to everyone—even to two people attending the same 'consciousness-raising workshops' and their numerous offshoots—is not at all possible. Such people may use identical words, and nod in agreement at their common language, but their meanings are as different to each of them as are the views of the same tree to different people. If their meanings are identical, they are then as mechanistic as Angstrom-Unit duplications. And as with the actual colour, and not with its Angstrom-Unit mechanistic description, so much depends upon the individual's acuity, experiences and needs, if you will, within the complex areas of awareness and all that that implies.

THOUGHT AND ACTION
. . . *a mishmash of gibberish* . . .

Opinion and thought are not synonymous. Opinion may be the product of thought; but thought is a far more continuing evolving process than is opinion. We say that someone is 'opinionated'; we surely don't mean that that person is 'thoughtful.' And we are surrounded by opinion, and thought is a very small island in a very large sea — a sea of opinion. Yet it is the island upon which human life is founded.

Our schooling system is not designed to teach, or even encourage, people to engage in independent thinking or even to think at all. Thinking itself is held in quite eccentric regard; and thinking as organic to the processes of being and becoming has little currency in this world of practicalists and pragmatists. Yet what is more 'practical' than clear thinking?

Nevertheless we keep going to the technologists for their expert opinions for solutions to our problems and for answers to our questions. But are our problems and questions only, or all, technological? I doubt that very much indeed. Yet it is we who have given the experts and technologists their power, and their power over us; it is we who rush to seek their opinions; and they have been zealous in seizing the opportunities we offered them. 'Thinkers,' by the very nature of 'thinking,' are rather introspective and retiring. Perhaps they need to be more aggressive in pressing their views and their thoughts, and more demanding of a 'fair share of the hearing.' Would they then continue to be 'thinkers'? I rather doubt that too.

Nevertheless, I believe there is more thinking now going on by so-called 'ordinary' people than ever before because events are so compelling these days that people must surely find themselves pondering and puzzling over them. Surely it behooves the public thinkers, who say they do so, to offer the best of their thinking to those who ponder and puzzle. And yet there is such an overburden of what is called 'thinking,' such a mishmash of gibberish, such an unclarity, that people who are indeed pondering and puzzling are being offered very little assistance. They are being told *direc-*

tions they should follow, as though thinking were only an operations manual.

More people are more glib now than ever before; yet more people are more puzzled than ever before. I've noted, as surely you have, how people of 'higher' schooling, for instance, and of expert opinions, are quite fluent; but their 'thinking,' while even broad-ranging, is quite imprecise, even shallow; while many people who have not been subjected to such 'higher' schooling may not be so fluent or so wide-ranging, but their ponderings and puzzlements are quite deep and forthright. Is it possible, I wonder, that those of fluency and expertise rationalise more than do the others? Is it possible that our schooling systems dilute independent thought and encourage rationalisation? Is it possible that people of 'higher' schooling and expertise have been more indoctrinated in terms of techno-language and techno-opinions which have become the substance of many disciplines with their expertise-sounding jargons in medicine, engineering, sociology, psychology — whereas those who are free from educational indoctrinations are also more free to think more clearly?

There is a practicality to clear thinking, to critical thinking, which the public 'thinkers' have misshapen to their own ends. Yet the practicality itself does not fade. We often hear, and lauditorily too, of 'opinion-makers.' But we don't laud, or even hear of, 'thought-evokers.'

People who are called, and especially those who call themselves, 'experts' or 'scientists' have for many years made me feel sand-gritty; mainly because such people, in my view, much too often stand in the way of 'clear thinking' *by others*. Their opinions, given with expertise and assurance, can indeed actually hamper the clear thinking of others. And we have all allowed this to happen to our selves through our indiscriminate dependence upon experts and opinion-makers. Perhaps now, surrounded as we are by an encroaching and uncalm sea of opinion, and by increasing numbers of the puzzled and the ponderers, we can indeed hope for more clear thinking on the part of more people.

When we talk of people 'awakening,' isn't this one of the things that is meant? I would surely *think* so.

HOW WE INTERPRET OURSELVES
. . . our human understanding of self . . .

We are all essentially interpretive beings and subject to all sorts of promises and threats; yet the individual human ascent is not subject *totally* to these promises and threats. We all possess some intimate hope that the good will emerge — somehow. Within some of us this is a conscious hope; within some of us it is a desperate hope.

Conscious or desperate or in oscillation between them, it would be useful to us if we would realise that central to all our individual emergences toward the good is our human understanding of self — not particularly in a psycho-analytical or sensorial manner but more especially through a deepening understanding of self in interrelationship with everything we as individuals recognise as being part of our private and public worlds. And this 'everything' is different for virtually each of us.

'Everything' is such a large word and there surely are things within this 'everything' which we may not know about or recognise or give any thought to, yet which affect us positively or negatively in ways both gross and subtle. Even so, who can know 'everything'?

Realising that we cannot know 'everything' makes it even more important for us to recognise and know the baselines of our references from which we interpret many things, precisely because we are essentially interpretive beings. If, for instance, one of our baselines of reference is belief in God and Church we can, in comfort, interpret many things as being 'the will of God' and not the will of Man. If one does not believe in God and Church (which are not necessarily synonymous at all, in my view) one can still have faith in Deity and interpret many things through belief in Divine intervention and Divine purpose. However, if one's frame-of-reference is belief in the concept of Deity as perhaps Man's greatest innovation, one's interpretations impose the greatest responsibilities upon Man himself as innovator. If, for instance, one of our baselines is belief in the *possible* continuation of life on our planet, we then interpret many of our own thoughts and actions, and the actions of others, within the context of the Man/

Earth interrelationship. If one of our baselines is that Man is doomed, our interpretation of events, and of our own lives too, is of quite a different order. If, for instance, one of our baselines of reference is belief in the hallowedness of all life while simultaneously recognising the enormous pressures stemming from overpopulation, our personal interpretations of our own responses in these areas become very complex, and do not lend themselves with any sort of personal integrity to glib slogans. For example: To believe in the hallowedness of all life would be one reason to be opposed to legalised abortion. To believe that population-pressures will strangle the planet would be one reason to be in favour of legalised abortion. Of course there are so many other reasons to be for or against legalised abortion; but the point here is that some baselines of reference are indeed very complex.

Yet it is probably valid to state that all our interpretations — the guides through which we live our lives and try to enhance the lives of others toward whom we have responsibility — stem from our baselines of reference. These may change for us from time to time as we become more aware or less aware of our understanding of self in relationship to our public and private worlds; as we become more intimately concerned or less concerned with our worlds, our selves, our senses of responsibility.

It behooves us to clarify in a continuous process of clarification our individual baselines of reference precisely because one of the human strengths is in our interpretive capability of many things.

ON IMMENSITY
. . . a larger scope, a deeper sense . . .

There is much within our private and public worlds over which to be disturbed, and many people of capability and goodwill have warned us for years of hazard. And yet, in my view, their effect remains not at all in proportion to their efforts. I've wondered, as perhaps many of you have, why is this so?

In my view, when public people of 'the good' maintain that they are trying to reach 'everyone' with their warnings and messages they delude themselves and their capabilities and us as well because 'everyone' is not reachable. Such people, often through their feelings of urgency, then dilute themselves into becoming facsimiles of Madison Avenue techniques in their attempts to reach 'everyone' and lose their earlier appreciation of the individual they seek to enrich with their thoughts — especially with their philosophical thoughts rather than only with their charts and exponential curves. Many of them then become cynical when they count on all people everywhere, or at least on a large majority, changing their errant ways of inner responses to self and to the world about them.

We are indeed in a world of more than 4,000-million people. What can 'everyone' mean in this context? Are you 'everyone'? Am I? Who is?

We are each of us individual human beings with our own histories, responses, conditionings, urgencies, optimisms, pessimism, visions, responsibilities, strengths of commitment — even our fingerprints are uniquely ours and no one else's, as is our genetic heritage. What is our least common denominator through which we *can* be reached? Or is there one?

I believe that each of us is surely capable of thought, of 'philosophical' thought, if you will, concerning our individual lives and of our 'place,' so to speak, within a world of thousands of millions of people. And we need to be addressed as individuals and not as a mass. Our thoughts are as individuals, and so are our responsibilities. This is our closest approach to any possible least common denominator.

In recent years more and more of us have come to view things in their immensity, which is very good indeed. Such a view offers us a larger scope, a deeper sense of self, of others, of our interrelated world, of many tangible and intangible matters. Such a view is an organic factor in our own evolvement and sense of 'place' and being. We have also begun to realise, increasingly, that many problems — fairly recent emergences within our consciousness — are *quite* immense. Because the many lines of communication and knowledge are more open and available, the immensity of the problems all about us becomes ever larger to us.

However, when we look for attempted solutions only in terms of immensity we become much smaller and weaker to our selves than we are or need to be. We then become depressed and pessimistic over immensity itself. Yet the largest mountain can be climbed only step by incremental step even if we can continue to see with each step that the immensity of the mountain remains.

The point here is this: Regardless of what we as individuals can do, immensity exists and the immensity of problems remains. If we close our minds to immensity we also close our selves away from concern regarding our individual 'place' within immensity, our individual understanding, our individual capability, and our individual recognition that we can be part of an incremental process within immensity toward the good.

And yet, when persuaders of 'the good,' especially of a particular solution in terms of population-pressures or food-supplies or various contaminations, attempt to reach 'everyone,' they offer one or another remedy in their public beliefs that the immensity of problems about which they are addressing a public will then be reduced in a sort of melting process. When they realise that the immensity remains and is not melting through the heat of their persuasions they become disheartened and feel their efforts to be wasted. We feel misled and also become disheartened over the immensity of the problems.

However, these persuaders of 'the good' have not addressed themselves to us as individuals and to our constant need to enrich our capabilities for deeper thought within the context of our philosophical selves. Yet we are nourished as individuals precisely through our philosophical selves. And it is through our philosophical selves that immensity does not become immobilising to us.

We can then confront many problems and view them in relationship with our own lives and with our deepened awareness of that ingredient which is incremental toward the good that each of us possesses.

ON QUESTIONS
. . . our demand for immediate answers . . .

What is our purpose? What are we for?

We are in a mania to find solutions, and we look at questions only in terms of possible answers. It is as if we want to see at least a glimmering of a recognisable answer before we will admit the question to our consciousness. We do not look at questions as questions containing their own validity. When we do look upon them and find no answer readily discernible to us and to those we label experts, we either reject the question out of hand or we say: 'Ah well, that's pretty philosophical,' and sigh with relief that we have found the proper label for it, the proper niche into which to cast that which disturbs us. Actually, 'philosophical' has become a catch-all term for many of those questions which we find to be too disturbing and demanding of our deep attention.

In fact, we have conditioned ourselves since The Bomb to expect answers. We have invested so much in so many phases of technology that we now demand and expect a proper return in terms of answers. In our expectations we become near-hysterical with a feeling of doom if answers are not readily forthcoming to questions of, for instance, population-pressures, energy-supplies, medical attentions, educational-system faultings, the goodlife—and a host of others less tangible.

In Medicine, for example, growing increasingly more costly to patients, physicians and administrators are discussing in ever widening circles the application of cost-benefit ratio techniques heretofore the province of industrial economics. An example here: A patient, 55 years of age, is diagnosed as requiring massive and costly surgery which could possibly extend his life by another year or perhaps two, during which he would require continuing medical attention. The question confronting physicians and administrators —and now still often asked of the patient—is whether or not the benefit to the patient is worth the cost. Such questions can be debated by physicians in a manner so that they can have their own built-in answers. Today, while we still hold the individual in some regard, the answer may be agonising to physicians. Several years ago the question itself would not have been raised by physicians.

Several years hence—if the mania to find answers continues and leads us further away from the individual and deeper into the mass—this question would indeed be answered through mechanised cost-benefit ratio applications. And yet, how could physicians even begin to attempt an answer to this question without first attempting to answer to themselves the question of the meaning of life? The question may not ever be answerable to them, but the need for its asking will surely educate them into becoming more humane as physicians and as individuals.

The idea that basic questions, deeply evaluated, can guide us in terms of *directions* toward solutions, toward possible solutions which enhance humaneness, seems increasingly unacceptable as though it were too slow a process in our age of haste and urgency. And we brought this age upon ourselves through our demand for immediate answers.

The 'answer' to basically difficult questions may be that there is no answer but only an everlasting direction *toward* an answer.

This in itself could dilute our fears of impotence and doom because it offers us, if we accept the offering, a sense of the on-goingness of our lives. It relieves us of being compelled to accept the answers, however awry, given for us to our basic questions, and strengthens the processes of our own autonomy.

Realising that the mania for answers is indeed a mania which can imprison us we *can* immunise ourselves against this mania through the recognition that to so many questions there can be no immediate acceptable answer but only a lifelong quest as one of the richest processes we possess in our human estate.

THE INUNDATING DATA-PILE
. . . *useful for extraction purposes* . . .

I should like to draw a verbal cartoon. A man studying a heavy book, a tome if you will, is standing beside a cornucopia, a horn, expelling a constant stream of information even while the rising data-pile already reaches his chest, and he needs to hold his book high above his head in order to study it. A caption should not be needed, but if one were wanted, perhaps the single word 'Dilemma' would suffice.

And of course it is quite a dilemma. What is to be done with this mounting data-pile? No sooner do we begin to make certain connections from information we already possess in our attempts to study and evaluate the whole, so to speak, than another newer piece of information swamps us. How can we evaluate what we already know if we believe that somewhere hidden in the constant piling of data is a particular piece of information which will modify all our past knowledge *which we have not yet evaluated*? And once we get this particular piece, should we keep on searching the pile for other pieces? To what aim? In the belief that knowledge is merely a collection of pieces of information? Yet the data-pile continues to increase, nearly endlessly it would seem.

Is there any resolution to this dilemma? Well, information is often surely useful, occasionally not; and more often than we are willing to admit quite repetitive, equivalent to the research technician who again and again — ten thousand times — boils distilled water at atmospheric pressure and finds the boiling-point to be 100-degrees Centigrade. And then, at the ten-thousandth-and-one 'experiment,' if you will forgive the expression, notes with surprise that the water begins to boil at 90-degrees Centigrade. What does he then do? Does he check his instruments to establish their accuracy, or does he fire off a project-proposal to the Ford Foundation?

One resolution to this dilemma of the constant stream of data, of the man in the cartoon, is this in my view: The data-pile is not a prime source for knowledge, for the finding of intelligent connections. It is useful for extraction-purposes, for the extraction from the pile of that data which one needs in one's quest for knowledge. The data-pile is equivalent to a dump to which all sorts of things are constantly added — and I don't mean this in any pejorative manner because dumps serve many useful purposes, indeed essential ones. But in order to find the dump-materials of some benefit one needs to approach it with some forethought already in mind, unless one happens to be a miscellaneous collector of all sorts of trivia, either for the sake of trivia or because one hopes to find some uses some day for the bits and the pieces.

The man in the cartoon obviously is seeking knowledge, and with some forethought. The steady stream of data which is nearly submerging him interferes quite actually with his search to make intelligent connections. He needs to extract himself from the pile, even while knowing of its existence and its potential value to him whenever he finds that he needs to acquire some pieces of data which may apply, positively or negatively, to his search for knowledge. He may find what he believes he needs within the data-pile, and he may not. But the pile itself does not then immobilise him, precisely because he is not dependent upon it for his continuing attempts to make intelligent connections, knowing full well that regardless of the mass of the data-pile it is only he, as an individual, who is capable of making these connections.

KNOWLEDGE FOR THE SAKE OF—WHAT?
. . . an avalanche of information, not of knowledge . . .

'Knowledge for the sake of knowledge' now seems to be one of those meaningless phrases with which we have been afflicted for years, especially when for too long 'knowledge' has been synonymous with 'information.'

Are we overloaded with information past the point of our absorbability? Is too much information simply being hurled at us? We are surely in an age more of information than of knowledge, more of data than of understanding. We are being swamped not because we are in what is called an 'information overload' as much as we are in a knowledge 'underload.' And the difference between knowledge and information is becoming increasingly more significant to us.

To me knowledge may lead to understanding which, in turn, may lead to clarity within our selves in terms of our many past, present and possible inter-connectednesses—a clarity which can enhance our sense of potency within the immensity in which we live to enable us to become individually aware of many insights within the many meanings of existence.

Information of itself may be interesting; it may be only bits of trivia. But information is often needed to enhance our knowledge which itself can be used or abused. When used, knowledge can enlarge our clarity; when abused, knowledge can be corruptive, even dangerous. For instance: Knowledge of binary bio-chemistry can lead military laboratory research people deliberately to bypass laws outlawing bio-chemical warfare devices by constructing two separate chemical substances, each of which is non-poisonous and 'legal'; and when these two are placed in adjoining compartments inside a bomb and the bomb released, in its fall the membrane separating the two non-poisonous substances is shattered, and the substances combine to form a deadly bio-chemical bomb which has been outlawed. Through the abuse of knowledge such warfare devices are indeed being made—in actual circumvention of the law by employees of the government which formulated the law. In this example it was not the data which were abused, or the information, but the *knowledge* of binary bio-chemistry.

Data are sterile. They need interpretation, then application of one datum to another, and these lead to that area called 'information.' Information when applied—that is, when connections are made within the various informations, so to speak—*may* contribute to knowledge. However, the information may not at all lead to knowledge; the information may be simply information—at a dead end. When it is at a dead end, and ever more is added to it, it then becomes an overload.

And so much to the point here: The ability of an individual to utilise information depends upon his or her desire and pre-requisite, if you will, *for* knowledge.

To add information only to other information and the combination again only to other information is an exercise in futility and a waste of resources. In terms of that phrase: 'Knowledge for the sake of knowledge,' when knowledge is applied only to other knowledge, and the combination again applied only to still other knowledge, knowledge itself becomes inbred, hazy, containing little clarity. And many people prefer haziness as self-protection, because clarity is in many ways indeed difficult to achieve and retain in confrontation with a world more of information than of knowledge.

But clarity has more than only one facet. Seeing clearly only what is external, what is outside one's self, is only part of clarity. One also needs clarity within self. When these two clarities merge, the unity-of-clarity is then possible. Without this merging, this unity, some sort of inner split occurs.

When clarity embraces an inner sense of self *and* beyond-self it adds to potency even as immensity itself is brought into sharper focus, perspective and scale. When knowledge is 'for the sake' of clarity, knowledge then reaches out to embrace our immense Universe, and our potentially immense selves, whatever 'universe' and self mean to us individually in our ever changing lives.

―――――――――

ON WISDOM
. . . *the puzzle of the human mystery* . . .

When one accepts a 'Divine Purpose' to one's life one can then guide one's life in terms of this purpose. The ancient scholars, for instance, accepting as the foundation of their beliefs the existence of an all-knowing Deity from whom all Universe-order flowed, used their efforts to generate wisdom aimed toward this belief.

Perhaps I could put it this way: The Ancients accepted the God-given order of the Universe as a basic premise. But ever since Kepler and Newton, mankind began to seek *a rational order* within the Universe. Those who followed them also began to question whether or not order did indeed exist; if it did, what were the implications to them in terms of Deity and in terms of wisdom? If it did not exist, what were the implications?

My point here is this: Many speak of 'the wisdom of the Ancients, of the ancient scholars, now hidden from us, a wisdom which can solve many problems and answer many questions if only we can uncover what they knew in certain esoteric areas.

Of course the Ancients had a wisdom most useful to them in their time and in their place. It was a wisdom with a pre-set goal, with an accepted life-purpose. And many of the things they did and wrote about then fell into place for them.

Today if one accepts a Divine Master Design or reincarnation or heaven or hell, one's map-of-life, so to speak, is quite clear before one. One's *inquiry* is also clearly mapped for one. And of course it is a comfort to be able truly to accept the belief that our actions do not stem from us but from Higher Authority before whom we can lay down our burdens at the end of the day and our many days; and we are therefore only rafts flowing along the River-of-Life and going wherever the stream takes us.

But we are not the Ancients anchored in their beliefs and with deep personal security in their knowledge. We have more diverse and more complex knowledge but we are unanchored; we remain afloat in space. We've not yet found our 'new place' in all of Nature. And we need to find this place; at least we need to seek it if we are not to remain adrift.

Our inquiries, despite moon-walks and space-probes, are more broad than deep. We seem to be trying to put together a technological puzzle, not the puzzle of the human mystery. The Ancients had an answer, an accepted answer, to the human mystery, and many-many things fell into place for them straightaway. We, with our expanded knowledge, cannot accept the same answer—we are different people everywhere on Earth—and many-many things do not fall into place for us. They may never fall into place for us ever again.

Perhaps through our sophisticated knowledge and techniques we have lost our simplicity, our one-to-one relationship with life and death. I would resist thinking so. I accept the complexity of our world, and our need to become ever more complex—but not at the cost of our total loss of simplicity and the profundities within simplicity.

What was, was; what is, is. We can't ever go home again unchanged. We cannot return to ancient wisdom however much we can and need to learn from it. But we learn in our present selves; we don't learn yesterday or tomorrow.

When wisdom becomes a method of reaching a preconceived

goal (as with the Ancients so secure in their beliefs) such 'wisdom' becomes measurable; and by a quirk organic to all measurement, it also becomes quite limited.

Today we seek mainly for such limited 'wisdom' and for the strangest of reasons, in my view. Capable of sending forth an astonishing Deep Space probe, we seem to exhaust ourselves in such a project in terms of our inquiries and we feel that so long as our ultra-sophisticated *device* is out there probing for us, we don't need to probe for our selves. A surrogate sort of bifurcation takes place here. We send some *thing* deep out there to explore for us while we sit, actually and metaphorically, watching it on television. To continue the analogy: We don't go along with it; we stay behind controlling it, and in our own comfortable surroundings. Our thoughts are not in space; they are of the *device* in space.

In many strange ways we are more Earth-bound than the Ancients. But with our expanding knowledge, still expanding in many ways, we cannot and dare not remain only Earth-bound in our thoughts and in our attempted understanding of our selves.

WHY SOME 'EXPERTS' ARE HARMFUL
. . . the mannered persuasionists . . .

The nuclear weapons issues, and others too, have been reduced to technicalities—a reduction foreshortening us in the present, and foreshortening our views, perspectives and scales of our own future and that of the human continuum.

Within technicalities expertise dominates. And experts—a term I often use rather pejoratively—by the very nature of expertise, are inbred and function within designated areas of self-chosen or assigned responsibility. (The Lodges may have spoken only to the Cabots, and while the Cabots replied, they said they spoke willingly to the only Higher Authority they recognised as being worthy of them.)

Expertise is, of course, very important *in certain areas,* in technological areas. For instance, one does want an expert surgeon, an expert mechanic, an expert engineer. But one wants them because one has a need for their expertise. This is all quite straightforward. Good experts are indeed needed. The problem arises here when one misunderstands the role of the expert; when one looks to experts to determine the substance of one's thinking. For instance: Experts often disagree in their opinions regarding the same matter in question. Who then is the evaluator? who judges between them? and from what non-expert frame-of-reference? It is more than only the fact that one expert often cancels another expert's opinion, precisely because the matter in question, the issue, still remains—often obscurely. Even when experts agree, the matter in question often remains obscure in the minds of non-experts precisely because the issue may not at all be resolvable through expert opinions. If it is a question of the *persuasiveness* of the expert, of the *manner* in which he presents his expert opinions, is it then his expertise which is listened to, or is it his manner? And so much of our world is a world of mannered persuasions.

Furthermore, people in authority who make decisions affecting us all depend upon expert opinions for the determination of policies. They often, quite naturally, give more credence to those experts whose opinions bolster the preliminary decisions which those in authority would like to make; and they give less credence to those experts whose opinions may be contrary. This is quite logical, even unavoidable. And good experts often serve a most essential purpose because they can be very valuable. However, what all too often happens is that the decision-makers have already succumbed to the imperatives of the technicalities. When this happens they are already past the point of moral/ethical/philosophical considerations and imperatives. They may attempt to couch their decision-making in moral/ethical/philosophical considerations and imperatives, but even these have been reduced to technicalities, if you will; these are no longer ideals or principles but rather persuasion-techniques.

We are indeed in a world of complex technicalities. And yet, if we-the-people are to determine policy, even theoretically, regarding complex issues, the question rises in awe before us: From what frame-of-reference are we-the-people to make these judgments? If dependence upon experts determines policy and the shape of Democracy, and if we cannot all become experts, what then of Democracy? Are we moving ever closer to a Technocracy? not only in the public and political sector but also in the private and intimate sector of our own responses, our own individuality and uniqueness-to-self. The recognition of the value, of the essentiality, of individual thought when in uncertain and confused confrontation with conflicting expertise is one of the cornerstones of Democracy—*and of individual autonomy.*

That individual thought is held in low repute, and often even in contempt (as when someone says: 'So who made you the expert?' or 'What makes you an authority?') continues to be costly, and it is becoming much too costly . . .

The denigration of 'philosophy' with its moral/ethical baseline-of-reference can destroy us. The recognition of its essentiality, and all that that means, may yet be able to save us.

And, save us from what? and *for what?*

MAN, THE LIVING END
. . . *violent master-terms we use* . . .

It is difficult for us not to think of ourselves as being the 'highest' organism in all of Nature. We are surely that to ourselves. It is when we think that because we are the 'highest' we are thereby the 'masters' of Nature that we get into all kinds of difficulties with ourselves and with all of Nature.

For instance: A master who does not have a functioning sense of his responsibility stemming from morality and ethics can readily become a harsh dictator, a driver of slaves who are considered by him to be lower in human qualities than himself—indeed, sub-human. He can then readily consider other organisms of Nature, other organic members, to be sub-lives for him to use or abuse as he sees fit. Such a master gives little thought to the inescapable reality of the interrelationship of all life, of the inter-connectedness of all life. We condemn master-race ideologies within our own species but give little thought to such ideologies as they affect other living organic members of life-giving Nature.

I am not anthropomorphising here; I am not endowing human characteristics upon non-human organisms. Not that at all. A whale is not a human, as a human is not a whale. It is the *gradations* which we impose upon other life — that we are the 'highest' and other life is thereby 'lower' or 'lowest' — that is the core of one of our many difficulties in any attempt we make to understand our own *place* in all of Nature. *We* cannot be what we are if other organisms — from the largest to the smallest — cannot be what *they* are; if we continue to interfere with what they are; if we continue to impose our human mastery upon life not human. Man is a symbiotic organism; indeed, all life is symbiotic — inter-dependent and inter-connected. It is simply impossible for Man to be the *only* living organism on this or any other planet. When will we note the obvious — and learn from it, as we must?

Yet we continue to speak of the 'conquest' of Nature; despite *some* ecological awareness we continue to plan for the 'exploitation' of the sea and all it contains as *'our* last frontier' in terms of *our* selves. Such violent master-terms we use in expressing our inter-connectedness with all life! And often we use them quite thoughtlessly and with little apparent malice.

For instance: A prominent geo-oceanographer — in the first of a series of articles prepared by the University of California for wide newspaper distribution as an instructional course, and funded by a grant from the National Endowment for the *Humanities* — wrote: 'Nothing could be worse for mankind — or the sea — than a lawless technological race' for the exploitation of the oceans. My question is: Would a law*ful* technological race for the exploitation of this 'last frontier' be the 'best' for mankind — or the sea?

I ask myself again and again: Why don't people — especially those of good intent and apparently well-equipped to do so — why don't they make the necessary connections in terms of the interlocking 'chain of life'? Why don't they realise that our responsibility is indeed to all of Nature and not only to our human selves?

One reason for this is the fact that we seem unable to accept another organic member of Nature on its terms and values in symbiotic harmony with ourselves. We anthropomorphise it, or we condemn it to a lower order.

In terms of our life, our individual life too, considered by us to be the 'highest,' we quite apparently believe that the 'chain of life' ends with us. We seem to believe—and *act* as though we do believe —that we are the living end.

ON ANTHROPOMORPHISING
. . . we are the translators . . .

Anthropomorphising defines the ascribement by us of human attributes to things and beings not human. We anthropomorphise non-human mammals, especially those we have domesticated. We do so with endangered whales and seals, with birds, flowers, trees, with the land itself. We anthropomorphise in many ways and in different degrees, and in doing so we reveal much of our autobiographical selves.

Anthropomorphising is a unique and ancient human characteristic in man's attempt to understand and find the unity of all things and beings. In earlier times it served a necessary purpose in the human ascent. But with the increased knowledge available to us, anthropomorphising is no longer adequate for us to comprehend the organic unity to *us* of all things and beings on our life-giving Earth. We have our own human language—constantly in need of refining and expansion; and other things and beings have *their* own language, so to speak. For us to understand them as to grasp their meanings and importances to us, we need to expand *our* language to understand *theirs*. And we cannot do so through our giving human attributes to things and beings not human because, no matter how much we anthropomorphise, we do not change the nature of other things and beings—we cannot give human qualities to other life, which has its own qualities, which we need to understand. Are we then to seek a sense of unity only with other life to which we *can* attribute human qualities and to reject everything to which we cannot give our own attributes?

It is human to anthropomorphise. *What* is anthropomorphised, and how this is expressed internally to self and externally through one's actions and responses are important ingredients here. They are becoming increasingly more important to us because we are so rapidly approaching the harsh reality that we need to make some very difficult choices if human life—and Earth itself and all it contains—is indeed to continue and to evolve.

We need to realise—and with a sense of urgency—that we need to make our own lives more humane, not because we are the *givers* of human qualities to other life but because we are the translators and evaluators into our own language of *all* things about us. That the current terms of our language are descriptive mainly of things materialistic is very much to the point here; and the warnings of danger from our contaminations of language resulting so much from our self-interest are all about us.

In order to translate and evaluate we need to know the language of the original—of the life-giving Earth, for instance—as well as our own human and humane language. When we do not possess, and fail to expand and purify our human language, our translations and evaluations of other lives and beings devolve into something stereotyped and inadequate and worse. And it is then *this* maimed language which we ourselves use in discourse with others of our kind, and through which all sorts of inadequate—even harmful—public and private decisions toward all life are then reached.

We cannot be intelligent translators and evaluators of any non-human life into maimed human language, much less of non-human life of which we know little or nothing. It is extremely important for us to realise that we *do* anthropomorphise in these terms and, despite a sense of self-congratulation and even, perhaps, self-fulfillment, remain largely ignorant of what we are doing.

We need to learn the language of our life-giving Earth on which we live, interwovenly, with non-human things and beings; and to expand our own evolving language and, thereby, our understanding. We need not only to note the fall of the sparrow but also to evaluate its meaning to us. When evaluation is omitted, we become less than our human and humane selves in our vital need for evolvement, and continuum.

And we need to be ever-increasingly aware that we are indeed within the Age of Decision of utmost urgency; and that our remaining choices do depend upon the best within us within the context of our deeply intimate understanding of the translations we attempt to make of things and beings both human and non-human.

PLANT, ANIMAL AND HUMAN GENETICS
. . . a critical quest . . .

The historian Toynbee has lamented—in regard to quality, not numbers—that in our breeding of plants and animals we are godlike; but in our own breeding we are rabbit-like. The eugenicists of the late Nineteenth Century and early Twentieth had equivalent lamentations. Eugenics deals with attempts, through breeding, to 'improve inborn or hereditary qualities,' especially of human beings; while genetics is that branch of biology dealing with hereditary characteristics and variations. Both eugenics and genetics stem from the Greek root-word meaning 'to be born.'

Toynbee and others of equivalent persuasion are partially correct regarding the skilled breeding of plants and animals. But then, we believe that we know what plants and animals are for. We breed them for many *specific* reasons: basically to increase yield, in its many meanings. This increase often means that a particular plant-species needs to be bred in order to be more disease-resistant or frost-resistant or drought-resistant. Plants are often bred or cross-bred in order to make their usable products more palatable, or in order to hasten their maturing-processes. Animals are bred for equivalent purposes, or for certain conformations considered by breeders to be desirable, or for speed and stamina. Such breeding of plants and animals often does result in the desired characteristics.

All such breeding involves the factor of domestication. This means that such plants and animals become more dependent upon human beings for their survival and continuation. For instance: The wild turkey, before its domestication, was considered to be a rather intelligent animal; today's turkey, many times meatier than its forebears, is a rather stupid animal and quite incapable of taking care of itself without human intervention and control. In breeding into it what *we* wanted — greater and quicker yield — we bred out of it its original capability for survival; and its survival is now dependent upon us. The same is so of the milk-producing cow, of hybrid corn, of domesticated decorative flowers — of all sorts of plants and animals.

Indeed, in the belief that plants and animals are to serve *us,* we have bred in characteristics we believe to be beneficial to us, and bred out those we believe to be harmful to us. And so we do appear to ourselves to be more-or-less godlike in our breeding of plants and animals — at least for the moment. The fact is that increased yield, in its many forms, is very much dependent upon us and, increasingly, upon our synthetic manipulations.

When Toynbee and others of his attitudes in this area draw breeding comparisons between human beings and other life they omit one basic complex factor: namely, that while skilled geneticists and breeders believe they know what plants and non-human animals are for, they do not know what they or we are for. Until they are quite certain they know what human beings are for, such breeding comparisons are puerile, foolish, and dangerous. And — can we ever know, with certainty, what we are for? What can 'yield' and its quality mean when applied to human beings? What *can* be our baselines-of-reference here? At one time such questions may well have been considered to be abstract, and of little direct effect upon individuals and the human continuum.

However, precisely because we are technologically capable — and increasing our capability — of manipulating many of the human genetic components, to seek to know what Man is for has now become a critical quest affecting our lives and our substance, our present and our future. And if we ever should be able to know what we are for, I believe we would also know that we are not for genetic manipulation.

PATHOGENS
. . . we cannot extricate ourselves . . .

If we believe — and act in the belief — that all life in all Nature has merit or demerit through us, because of us, we lack an essential ingredient vital to our understanding of life and of our selves. Through this lack we can readily convince ourselves that everything, but everything, exists for us. Let us assume that everything does exist for us. If so, for what do we exist? Surely for more than only existence itself.

A basic principle in all living things is that life seeks to live, not to die; and to live is to be able to overcome anti-life obstructions. This applies to humans as well as to bacilli. Consider the fact that many diseases generate an immunity against man-made attempts to control them. Penicillin, for instance, was highly successful against gonorrhea, and for years. Now there is a strain of gonococcus bacterium which is both highly virulent and immune to penicillin. Even the bacterium seeks to live and not to die.

Yet it can be said that all life stems from prior decay. Life-giving soil, for instance, is a product of earlier and continuing decay of living matter, decayed mainly through the effects of living microorganisms, of soil bacteria which, in turn, themselves decay. If all living things once alive existed forever, there would be neither place nor need for generations of living things; and there would be neither place nor need for us, in our generation, and for our progeny. Life would then be unchanged and in a condition of biological stasis, of standing still, of non-evolvement.

The point here is this: Within biology life follows the paths of most resistance or perishes. The higher the organism in terms of biological complexity, the more it does need to follow the paths of most resistance if it is not to perish. A simple bacterium strain, or an earwig strain, could live for many thousands of generations unchanged, but the complex human organism cannot. Because life seeks to live and not to die, pathogenetic organisms, disease-causing organisms, become part of the processes of the most-resistance factor essential to life's evolvement, especially of more complex organisms. Without pathogens there would be no complex organisms in Nature; indeed, we would not be if not for the obstacles we needed to overcome. And we *will* not be if we do not overcome growing obstacles both natural and man-made.

In simpler times the man-made obstacles were simpler and the natural ones more complex; and Darwinian implications of the survival through adaptation of the biologically fittest applied in large measure. Today the natural obstacles are much simpler than the man-made ones, surely in comparison. The man-made obstacles we have generated are not at all simple.

The paths of most resistance are now mainly against obstacles of our own making. This in itself is difficult to admit — to recognise. One of these obstacles is indeed the belief that everything exists for us. This, quite probably, is a basic obstacle, a basic skewness in our philosophical attitude, if you will. Perhaps all life does exist for us, perhaps all life does not exist for us. And yet, because we affect virtually everything, we cannot extricate ourselves from responsibility *for* everything. And we need to evolve an enormous sense of both awareness and responsibility toward those obstacles of our own making. If we are not to perish through our man-made pathogens, so to speak, these are some of the central paths of most resistance we need to follow if we are ever to ascend, or even to survive.

ON RE-THINKING MANY THINGS
. . . *most critical angle of divergence* . . .

In a world now containing 4,000-million individual human beings generalisations about 'mankind' and 'the human condition,' and even 'human nature' are banal. Such generalisations reduce us to the biological level of life, to the species level; they do not raise us to the height of individual awareness, individual responsibility, individual 'spirituality' (regardless of our definition of this word), individual need for wisdom. (Ninety-nine percent assurance of *anything* is meaningless if you are the unassured 1%; to you un-assurance is 100%.) There are now so many 'for thems' in the world, but only one 'for me' and only one 'for you.' This is important to realise in our crowded world in which people are becoming more clone-like in terms of response.

(Cloning is a biological technique for the reproduction of many identical offspring from a single cell. A herdsman who decides to clone his best-producing cow in order to have a herd of a hundred or a thousand 'best-producing' cows identical to the original would find that he has made a fatal error because any single infection would infect his entire clone-herd precisely because there would be no *individual* variation and resistance among the clones.)

Does the human mind and spirit contain a built-in evolving need for wisdom? for an attempt to embrace the unity of self and Universe? From whence did this need emerge? Is it evolving or devolving or both? I do not believe that it comes from Divinity, which I consider to be one of Man's greatest innovations. Divinity as an answer is much too simplistic in our complex and intertwined world. And what quality of inner strength does wisdom bring to bear within the individual? The questions are many . . .

I believe that human destiny (there is no smaller word here) is now at its most critical angle of divergence. We have made it so. This destiny can go upward or downward. That it may go both upward and downward, and muddle through somehow, is not the point. We have fabulous quantities of knowledge and data, yet we are going downward; and the slide will continue so long as we continue to depend upon quantitative thinking. (While it is not possible to live *only* qualitatively, it is horrendously possible to live only quantitatively. Understanding this difference, and the multiple areas affected through such understanding, is now utterly essential.)

Are we to depend upon 'Nature' to bail us out through famine or pandemic virulences for which there will be no antidotes? Are we to depend upon the cruelty in 'human nature' to destroy through war or *triage* half the world's population, leaving the other half 'free' to continue its insanities? What does such dependence do to us *now* in terms of our own thinking and in terms of our own spirit?

We need to re-think many things — not only Science and Philosophy, or life and death, or rationality and a-rationality, or population-pressures and a limited planet . . . and so on—so that we may possibly be able to see, through enhanced vision and evolved perspective, what we are for, what life is for. And, thereby, enrich not only our selves in the moment but also the human continuum.

However complexly interwoven, the panorama before us contains many aspects of sighted hope (as opposed to blind hope) stemming from the human individuality and totality in the present, and the human capability for evolvement into the long foreseeable future.

ON THE ENDANGERMENT OF OUR SPECIES
. . . a missing ingredient . . .

Can mankind save itself as an endangered species?

There is little question that if we continue along our present paths we will accelerate our own extinction—perhaps not in our lifetime but surely within a time presently conceivable to us.

I see no possibility of any 'technological breakthrough' which could slow the downward slide. My reason for thinking so is this: The paths of technological 'progress,' so well defined during the past three decades, lead only to further technological 'progress' in a linear manner—and this kind of progress, if continued, will destroy us and the planet. Technology will certainly perform enormous achievements in the future, as it has done in the past. But there is a missing ingredient in all these performances which technology itself—no matter how sophisticated and widespread throughout the world—simply cannot supply. It is beyond technology's realm, and cannot be found along technology's paths.

I am not referring to the cost technology abstracts from Earth's limited resources and the usually toxic residues resulting from technology's 'progress,' but to an ingredient which could, and should, be in everlasting supply. I am referring to the fact that while Man is a biological organism united—at least so far as atoms are concerned—to all other organisms and inorganic matter on

Earth and in the Universe, he is now more than only a biological organism. So much more, indeed, that he may be considered as a separate, a *distinctly* separate species.

The missing ingredient so imperative for our survival is our ethical evolvement, our recognition of our species-difference, and our acceptance of this difference as a gift, a challenge, and a special responsibility.

It is said that we use only 2-to-5 percent of our cranial capability. I should like to ask what percentage of our ethical capability are we using? Educational projects are involved with increasing the use of our minds. No projects are involved with increasing the ethical/moral use of our mind/body complexity. What of the 'Spirit of Man' which is, quite apparently, traveling a course becoming estranged from his technological path? Can the two paths meet? If they cannot, we will hasten our extinction. If they can, what is needed for their union?

In my view, what is basically needed is a conscious attempt at understanding what the Ideal means to us as individuals—what Idea itself means. Not in terms of utility, of use, of measurability, but in terms of the philosophical importance of Idea and Ideal, of the humane-ethical-aesthetic vitalness to us of these two words. In considering their importance and what they mean, we do not abrogate 'realism' but embrace it. While aware of our human failings, we become aware of our capability to correct them—at least, in some measure.

I realise that 'philosophy' has become a pejorative word to many, especially to impatient activists much of whose activism, conducted without adequate knowledge, wisdom or idea, has proved to be ineffectual and self-defeating. More than short-sighted activism, more than technology in its most sophisticated achievements, it is philosophy which can help us understand something of our human meaning, our evolving human purpose and responsibility.

It is this kind of understanding—even our recognition of its necessity and our sincere endeavours toward it—that can join our fabulous technology to our even more fabulous Spirit of Man, rectify our current planetary schizophrenia, and insure our continuance for some time to come.

ON 'HUMAN NATURE'
. . . the basic good . . .

What is present within our human nature to preserve us from catastrophe? Or do we not possess anything organic within our human nature to preserve us and to enhance our own continuation on the planet into the long foreseeable future?

When we speak of 'human nature' we usually say 'But that's human nature.' We invoke 'human nature' as excuse, not as explanation. We simply never say 'But that's human nature' when referring to something noble within the human capability, as though we believe the noble to be external to human nature. And strangely too, we never use this phrase when referring to something very evil, as though we refuse to accept the very evil as ever being part of our human capability against which we need to be ever alert. It is as though we believe the very evil to be a Satanic implant within us over which we cannot have human control, and of which we can rid ourselves not through our selves but only through some form of exorcism, of intercession by higher non-human Authority.

There are many who say 'You can't change human nature. Human nature doesn't change.' Do they believe that 'human nature' is the only ingredient of human life which has retained constancy and has been fixed for all time since the beginnings of the human emergence? And fixed by whom? by what? At which point in the human evolvement did 'human nature' become fixed?

We are each of us mind/body/emotional/spiritual complexities, evolving complexities upon our evolving Earth within our evolving solar system with its life-giving devolving Sun. Do we believe that of all aspects of life, 'human nature' is the one ingredient incapable of evolving; that it is a constant human frailty? But that's an absurdity which torsions Nature and Natural Law *and us within the now* in our attempts to grasp the implications to us, now, of our capacity for our ever-expanding reason and awareness, and of our inner hope that life indeed can and will continue on our Earth into the long future.

The basic good in human nature, as I see it, involves the individual's capability for projectability beyond the moment, beyond his action in the moment. This projectability makes it possible for us to recognise aspects of our selves of which we are *not* proud. Capable of sitting in judgment upon others and self, we are thereby capable of *attempting* to change even that which we may consider to be 'natural' to us, to our human self. We are, in short, capable of attempted transcendence beyond the moment, and we can indeed *attempt* to become more humane toward self and all life.

The basic good in human nature—our human capacity for projectability—makes it possible for us to understand more fully the astonishing variety and complexity within 'Nature,' and the astonishing complexity and variety within 'human nature,' and the wondrous complexity of the interrelationships between them. Both Nature and 'human nature' are constantly evolving, and occasionally devolving; and the complexity of their interrelationship increases daily.

And yet, it is within the individual human capability to understand this complexity, and to partake of its wonder, for the sake of our own evolvement in the moment, and for the evolvement of the human continuum beyond the moment.

I believe that the capacity for wonder—within this context—to be organic to the human nature of the human individual. And therein is one of the most potent seeds of hope for the enhancement of life on this, our life-giving planet.